The Study Hall Test Prepara

The Study Hall Test Preparation Book

*SAT is a registered trademark of the College Board, which was not involved in the production of, and does not endorse this product. *ACT is a registered trademark of ACT, Inc., which was not involved in the production of, and does not endorse this product.

studyhalldallas.com

The Study Hall Test Preparation Book

© Copyright 2016
Henry Davis

The Study Hall Test Preparation Book

`Instruction Contents

Introduction – pg 5
    Explanation of How the Program Works and Which Test to Take

Standardized Test Truths – pg 7
    Explanation of factors which apply to all stadardized test

Critical Reading – pg 8
    How to Read Critical Reading Passages – pg 8
    Types of Passages – pg 9
    Types of Questions – pg 9

Writing Skills – pg 11
    Common English Usage Rules Tested – pg 12
    Punctuation Rules – pg 15

Math – pg 21
    Averages – pg 21 & 32
    Percentages – pg 22
    Word problems – pg 22
    Inequalities – pg 23
    Absolute values – pg 23
    Exponents – pg 24
    Radicals – pg 25
    Simultaneous equations – pg 25
    Scientific notation – pg 26
    Angles – pg 27
    Area – pg 27
    Volume – pg 29
    Pythagorean Theorem – pg 30
    Special triangles – pg 31
    Congruent and similar triangles – pg 31
    Functions – pg 32
    Proportions & Ratio – pg 33
    Work problems – pg 34
    People moving problems – pg 35
    Exterior angle of triangle – pg 35
    Sum of 2 sides of a triangle – pg 35
    Statistics – pg 36
    Order of operations – pg 36
    Probability – pg 37
    X & Y intercepts – pg 37
    Abstractions – pg 37
    Split numerator – pg 38
    Overlapping groups – pg 38
    Shaded regions – pg 38
    Fraction within fraction – pg 39
    Remainders – pg 39
    Sequences – pg 40

The Study Hall Test Preparation Book

    Variation – pg 40
    Sine, cosine, tangent – pg 41 & 43
    Slope – pg 41
    Permutation and combination – pg 41
    Radians – pg 42
    Circle graph equation – pg 42
    Logarithms – 42
    Matrix – pg 42
    Distance rate formula – pg 43
    Domain and range – 43
    Imaginary mumbers – pg 43
    Complex numbers – pg 44
    Triginometric identities – pg 44
    Period – pg 45

ACT Preparation
    Structure and format – pg 47
    English Usage – pg 49
    Science – pg 50

SAT Preparation
    Structure and format – pg 59
    Math not on the ACT
        Vertex of parabolas – pg 60
        Complete the square – pg 61
        Quadratic formula – pg 61

Math Cues – pg 63

Idioms – pg 66

Words that are Commonly Confused - pg 67

The Study Hall Test Preparation Book

How does the Study Hall Test Preparation program work?

Since the SAT and PSAT have changed, the content tested almost exactly moirrors the comtent on the ACT. That allows us to rely more on improving reading, writing, and math content knowledge. We will identify any contnet gaps an individual student has and apply the appropriate remedy.

The **essential parts** of the program are:

Two one hour appointments during which the students get their text and **individual instruction** informing them about the **strategies and skills** required for the tests.

After the appointments, the students come in to **take sections of the tests**. Upon completion of a test section **we review** the tests and show them how to answer questions correctly. **Appointments are not necessary**.

After each full test, especially after the first full test, we **analyze each student's performance** and determine **specific content gaps**.

After we determine the content needs, whether it is with individual instruction, interactive instruction and practice, or supplemental materials **we improve the content gaps** if present.

The students return to the **test, analyze, and improve** cycle for **all the ACTs and SATs** they take **until they graduate**.

We are open seven days a week, and they **don't need appointments** to take the tests, so they can fit test sessions into their schedules conveniently. The students here get **exclusive access to our websites**. The students will find instructive videos, interactive math questions and reading passages and much more. We give them access to the mobile optimized webpages because kids these days expect information to be available 24/7. The main learning takes place onsite but the online program is proving to be a **very valuable tool since they can access it 24/7**.

The Study Hall Test Preparation Book

Which test should we take?

This is probably the most common question I get. We prepare students for both. Since the **SAT** has changed and is remarkably similar to the **ACT**, preparing the students for both will be relatively seamless.

The **ACT** is much more **time pressured** as the average time spent per question has to be lass than a minute (49 sec) whereas the **SAT** average time per question (1 min 10 sec) is a bit over a minute. That being said, we will be working on test taking skills and monitoring each student's needs to maximize his or her scores on the best test for her or him.

The principal reason we can't be 100% certain which test a student will do better on is that we cannot precisely replicate the testing conditions so that we know how a student will react to the severe time constraints students encounter in taking the ACT. We **prepare** the students here for **both tests** and coordinate the preparations.

The Study Hall Test Preparation Book

Standardized Test Truths

Read to Eliminate Answer Choices
The most important aspect when approaching stanardized tests and especially Critical Reading passages is that the test makers use the term "**Best Answer**." Before you leave this page laughing saying that obviously you want the best answer read on. The way the the test makers interpret that phrase is one of the keys to the test. This simple phrase gives them a wide latitude. They can give you **four bad choices**. You look at the choices and don't feel any are good. You're right, but one will be better than the other fthree.

The other thing this phrase does, and this is more frustrating, is allows them to give you **two correct answers**. You will look and say that "I could make a case for either of these two."You have to learn to tell why one is better than another. And that is what you are comparing, why one of the answers is better than the other. This "Best answer" strategy applies to all of the non math sections.

When you're in the reading section, one of the ways to improve performance is to look at the answers and try to **eliminate answer choices**. This way you won't be caught up defending a major choice, rather you look for the weakness of each of the answer choices and leave yourself the best choice. Frequently it is a matter of finding the one word which will eliminate a choice.

Use the Answer Choices
There is one more technique you can employ in the reading section. If you are stumped and can't come up with an answer, examine the **answer choices** closely. Determine if there are clues in the selection of answer choices available. For instance, are there three negative answers and one positive? What you are trying to determine here is if there are three choices that are related and one that is not related to the other three. Either way, you can use the answer choices as one last technique for pulling an answer out.

Bubbling in Answer Choices
-The typical way most students bubble in the answer choices is to finish one question, go to the bubble sheet and fill it in. Then solve the next question. Finish question 1, bubble in answer 1. Finish question 2, bubble in answer 2. And so forth.

This actually wastes a lot of time. You're distracting yourself between two distinct tasks - solving questions and bubbling in answers. This costs you time in both mental switching costs and in physically moving your hand and eyes to different areas of the test.

Here's a better method:
Solve all your questions first on each test page, then **bubble all of them in at once**. If you get well practiced at this method and feel comfortable with the time you have left you can solve all your questions first on the test pages, then bubble all of them in at once.

This has several huge advantages: you focus on each task one at a time, rather than switching between two different tasks. You also eliminate careless entry errors, like if you skip question 7 and bubble in question 8's answer into question 7's slot.

By saving just 10 seconds per question, you get back 200 seconds on a section that has 20 questions. This is huge.

The Study Hall Test Preparation Book

Critical Reading

Read the Questions First. Do not read the answers. That gets confusing. Before you read the reading passages, read the questions. This tells you what the passage is about, gives you an idea of what you are looking for, and, most importantly, how to attack that passage. And that is what you are doing with every one of the reading passages. You are attacking them. You are taking them apart to get points.

Reading the question over can also alert you to the types of questions you want to know about as you read the passage. These would be questions about the organization of the passage, about the role a paragraph played in the passage, or about techniques the author used in developing a passage or defending an argument.

Read the Passage In Detail, then Answer Questions
This method is what most students already use, If you encounter time problems you can use another method

Skim the Passage, then Read the Questions
This is one startegy commonly used.

Skim the passage on the first read through. **Don't try to understand every single line**, Just get a general understanding of the passage. You want to try to finish reading the passage in 3 minutes, if possible.

Next, go to the questions. If the question refers to a line number, then go back to that line number and understand the text around it.

If you can't answer a question within 30 seconds, skip it.

This skimming method works because the questions will ask about far fewer lines than the passage actually contains. For example, lines 5-20 of a reading passage might not be relevant to any question that follows.

By taking the opposite approach of going back to the passage when you need to refer to it, you guarantee reading efficiency. You're focusing only on the parts of the passage that are important to answering questions.

Critical Skill: You must be able to skim effectively. This means being able to quickly digest a text without having to slowly read every word. If you're not quite good at this yet, practice it if you have time problems.

Since we will be practicing the tests you candetermine which works best for you, based on test data

The Study Hall Test Preparation Book

Types of Passages

The ACT and SAT have predictable types of passages.
The **ACT** has Humanities, Prose fiction, Social studies, and Natural science passages.
The **SAT** has 1 passage concerning US and World Literature, 2 for History/Social Studies, and 2 for Science.

Other standardized tests may have similar types of passages, but those can be more unpredictable.

Types of Questions

You will find some **Factual** questions where they state:

"According to this passage . . .," or
"The following were addressed in the passage EXCEPT . . ."

In other words, three of the items were addressed in the passage and one of them was not. Factual questions are similar to factual questions you are used to in school. You can find the answers in the passage. They won't be verbatim like your textbooks, but the answer will be there.

Line Reference
When you are given a specific line reference type question, remember that the answer will rarely be evident from the information just on that line. You will need to read a few lines before the specified
line and a few lines after the specified line.

There are **Inference** questions. When you infer something you are taking a fact and drawing a deduction or inference from that fact. They ask two types of inference questions.

Author Logic or **Outside Inference** is where they are asking you to place the fact in context using common sense. This is where they may ask:

"The author would most likely agree that . . .,"or
"The paragraph that most likely precedes or follows would be .. ."

With this type of inference question you go outside the passage and see where the fact fits in a greater context. You can be, indeed need to be, logical in this case.

Implication questions are far more common and are where you are confined to infer or imply only from the passage. This is where it says

"It can be inferred from what the author wrote on line 52 that . . .," or
"From the way the word "up" was used in line 20, you can infer that it means......"

The Study Hall Test Preparation Book

In this case, you are confined to the use of the word or phrase in the passage. If they use "up" to mean "down" that's what you have to go with. For instance, they recently had a

passage about animals in captivity. You and I feel compassion for the animals. Several of the answer choices are of a compassionate nature. But the author of this passage was very objective, examining the good and the bad sides of captivity. You must dissociate yourself from your feelings and only answer according to the information as given in the passage.

When you have an implication or an inference question, ask yourself if they are confining you to the passage, or are they saying to go outside the passage. You'll see how that limits your answers immediately.

The answers to **Main Idea** questions are pretty predictable. An answer is going can be too broad, too general, covering more than the passage covers, too narrow, or unrelated but sounds good.

Be careful that you distinguish between the main idea and the most important point. Frequently the most memorable point made in a passage is identified as the main idea because it was dramatic or otherwise memorable, but it was not the main idea.

If you find yourself having problems determining the main idea of a reading passage, look at the beginning of the passage and in the last sentence or two of the passage and see if the topic discussed there doesn't leave you with a correct answer choice.

The questions about the **Attitude, Style, Tone, or Mood** of the passage are one's you can readily figure out with some practice. These are dull passages so the author tone will be dull. lok for qualifying words like "somewhat," "partially," or 'reservedly" as these qualifiers soften stronger, more emotional words, Terms that are emphatic, argumentative, controversial, or extreme are not likely to be correct.

The Study Hall Test Preparation Book

English Usage or Writing Skills

The **SAT** and **ACT** use **passage based questions**

The Question Format

And that is exactly the primary gripe against forgeries. Not only <u>did</u> they swindle money from the buyers,
                                    22
but also they belie our conception of reality itself. Our understanding of time and age is suddenly <u>ripped out</u> from
                                                                                                    23
under us, and our consequent anger is not surprising. But what is truly <u>mistaking</u> is the tendency to destroy known
                                                                        24
forgeries because of this anger. If the past's mistakes made way for improvements in the future, that would be enough to validate their consideration

22. A. NO CHANGE
    B. do
    C. do,
    D. do not

23. A. NO CHANGE
    B. rips out
    C. ripping out
    D. rip

You will be asked for the best choice for the underlined portion of the passage. Question 22 requires you to notice that "did" is correct until you encounter "belie" in the next line. "Belie" is in the present tense and we cannot change it. So we work backward and change "did" to B. do so that we keep the tense correct.

studyhalldallas.com

The Study Hall Test Preparation Book

Rules of English Usage

Now is the time to set aside your texting and email writing and get ready to dial up the accuracy of your grammar and punctuation. Remember that a subordinate clause is not Santa's helper; it's an element of written English you need to master - along with a few other facets of the language.

Fortunately, the test people are relatively predictable regarding which rules they will choose to quiz you about. While we will include a complete grammar and punctuation guide in the second part of this section, we will focus on the writing skills question most likely to appear on the test.

It is crucial that you realize in this section you are looking for the **best rendition** of the sentence. You may not be correcting a mistake. You may be selecting a better formulation of the sentence. You may choose active voice as opposed to passive voice. You may simply select a more direct phrasing.

Keep in mind **10% - 20%** of the time the sentence is **correct**.

There are a few grammar rules that you need to know for the writing skills section. Those crucial rules (the errors are underlined) are:

1. **Subject verb agreement**.
   - Along the white sand beach sits the beautiful condominiums. (sit is correct)

2. **Using the simple past verb form with a helping** verb, or **using a past participle form without a helping verb** (Keep in mind irregular verbs).
   - The security guard had gave us a real inspection when we tried to enter the museum. (gave is correct)

3. **Error in use of idioms**. .
   - The school officials were pleased with the attempt at attracting a highly respected instructor. (should be "to attract")

4. **Non idiomatic preposition** coming after a verb.
   - abide by
   - abide in
   - accuse of

3. **Wrong word**.
   - accept/except
   - adapt/adopt
   - affect/effect

4. **Wrong verb tense**.
   - Increased levels of air pollution causes many of our health problems. (should be "cause")

The Study Hall Test Preparation Book

5. **Number agreement**.
   - While the economies of Scandinavian countries and Great Britain are considered <u>an example</u> of success, they are too different to be considered together. (should be "<u>examples</u>")

6. **Pronoun in the wrong number**-be very careful of pronouns-a common question – error in number, case, shift in person or number, or ambiguous reference.
   - The typical college student has difficulty adjusting to academic standards much higher than those of <u>their</u> school. (should be "<u>his</u>")

7. **Pronoun in the wrong case** in the compound noun phrase.
   - My aunt and uncle join my parents and <u>I</u> for dinner every Thursday. . (should be "<u>me</u>")

8. **Pronoun shift** within a sentence.
   - One cannot sleep soundly if <u>you</u> exercise vigorously before retiring to bed. . (should be "one" or "<u>he or she</u>")

9. **Pronoun with an ambiguous reference**.
   - The United States entered into warmer relations with China after <u>its</u> compliance with recent weapons agreements. (should clarify which country "<u>its</u>" is referring to)

10. **Faulty comparisons**-things that can't be logically compared.
    - A Nobel Peace Prize winner and the author of several respected novels, Elie <u>Wiesel's name</u> is still less well known than last year's Heisman Trophy <u>winner</u>.

11. **Misuse of adjective or adverb**.
    - The applicants for low-interest loans hoped to buy <u>decent</u> built houses for their families. . (should be "<u>decently</u>")

12. **Double negative**.
    - James easily passed the biology exam <u>without hardly</u> studying his lab notes.

13. **Run on sentence**.
    - The decrease in crime can be attributed to a rise in the number of police officers, more than five hundred joined the force in the last year alone. (should have a semi-colon or period following "officers")

14. **Sentence fragment**.
    - While many office managers are growing more and more dependent on facsimile machines, others resisting this latest technological breakthrough.
    -

15. **Misplaced modifier**.
    - Flying for the first time, the roar of the jet engines intimidated the small child, and he grew frightened as the plane roared down the runway.

16. **Faulty parallelism**.
    - Nineteenth-century nihilists were concerned with neither the origins of philosophical thought nor how societal laws developed.   (the noun phrase following "neither" and "nor" should be parallel)

17. **Faulty coordination or subordination**.
    - Ben Franklin was a respected and talented statesman, and he was most famous for his discovery of electricity.

18. **Prefer the active voice**
    Incorrect: A decision was reached by the committee.
    Correct: The committee reached a decision.

19. **Use comparatives (comparing two things) and superlatives (comparing three or more things) with care**
    Incorrect: Which of these two brands of toothpaste is best?
    Correct: Though Shaw and Jackson are impressive, Hobbs is the most qualified of the three candidates running for mayor

Context Revision Questions

Concern with context   Be sure that the flow from one sentence to the next makes a logical transition. Pay attention to the move from one paragraph to the next one. Make sure the transition is smooth and makes sense.

Combine sentences-punctuation See where sentences can be combined to improve clarity. Likewise, see where a long sentence can be made into two shorter more direct sentences.

General organization understanding and the author's thinking Pay particular attention to places where the passage strays away from the main point the author is trying to convey. This error can be from an organizational or content standpoint.

The Study Hall Test Preparation Book

Punctuation

Comma

Use a comma in the following circumstances:

to join **2 independent clauses by a comma and a coordinating conjunction** (and, but, or, for, nor, so).

> Road construction can be inconvenient, but it is necessary.
>
> The new house has a large fenced backyard, so I am sure our dog will enjoy it.

after an introductory phrase, prepositional phrase, or dependent clause.

> To get a good grade, you must complete all your assignments.
>
> Because Dad caught the chicken pox, we canceled our vacation.
>
> After the wedding, the guests attended the reception.

to separate elements in a series. Although there is no set rule that requires a comma before the last item in a series, it seems to be a general academic convention to include it. The examples below demonstrate this trend.

> On her vacation, Lisa visited Greece, Spain, and Italy.
>
> In their speeches, many of the candidates promised to help protect the environment, bring about world peace, and end world hunger.

to separate nonessential elements from a sentence. More specifically, when a sentence includes information that is not crucial to the message or intent of the sentence, enclose it in or separate it by commas.

> John's truck, a red Chevrolet, needs new tires.
>
> When he realized he had overslept, Matt rushed to his car and hurried to work.

between coordinate adjectives (adjectives that are equal and reversible).

> The irritable, fidgety crowd waited impatiently for the rally speeches to begin.
>
> The sturdy, compact suitcase made a perfect gift.

after a transitional element (however, therefore, nonetheless, also, otherwise, finally, instead, thus, of course, above all, for example, in other words, as a result, on the other hand, in conclusion, in addition)

> For example, the Red Sox, Yankees, and Indians are popular baseball teams.
>
> If you really want to get a good grade this semester, however, you must complete all assignments, attend class, and study your notes.

with quoted words.

"Yes," she promised. Todd replied, saying, "I will be back this afternoon."

in a date.

October 25, 1999

Monday, October 25, 1999

25 October 1999

n a number.

15,000,000

1614 High Street

in a personal title.

Pam Smith, MD

Mike Rose, Chief Financial Officer for Operations, reported the quarter's earnings.

to separate a city name from the state.

West Lafayette, Indiana

Dallas, Texas

Avoid comma splices (two independent clauses joined only by a comma). Instead, separate the clauses with a **period, with a comma followed by a coordinating conjunction, or with a semicolon.**

The Study Hall Test Preparation Book

Semicolon

Use a semicolon in the following circumstances:

to join 2 independent clauses when the second clause restates the first or when the two clauses are of equal emphasis.

> Road construction in Dallas has hindered travel around town; streets have become covered with bulldozers, trucks, and cones.

to join 2 independent clauses when the second clause begins with a conjunctive adverb (however, therefore, moreover, furthermore, thus, meanwhile, nonetheless, otherwise) **or a transition** (in fact, for example, that is, for instance, in addition, in other words, on the other hand, even so).

> Terrorism in the United States has become a recent concern; in fact, the concern for America's safety has led to an awareness of global terrorism.

to join elements of a series when individual items of the series already include commas.

> Recent sites of the Olympic Games include Athens, Greece; Salt Lake City, Utah; Sydney, Australia; Nagano, Japan.

Colon

Use a colon in the following circumstances:

to join 2 independent clauses when you wish to emphasize the second clause.

> Road construction in Dallas has hindered travel around town: parts of Main, Fifth, and West Street are closed during the construction.

after an independent clause when it is followed by a list, a quotation, appositive, or other idea directly related to the independent clause.

> Julie went to the store for some groceries: milk, bread, coffee, and cheese.

> In his Gettysburg Address, Abraham Lincoln urges Americans to rededicate themselves to the unfinished work of the deceased soldiers: "It is for us the living rather to be dedicated here to the unfinished work which they who fought here have thus far so nobly advanced. It is rather for us to be here dedicated to the great task remaining before us — that from these honored dead we take increased devotion to that cause for which they gave the last full measure of devotion —

> I know the perfect job for her: a politician.

at the end of a business letter greeting.

> To Whom It May Concern:

The Study Hall Test Preparation Book

to separate the hour and minute(s) in a time notation.

    12:00 p.m.

to separate the chapter and verse in a Biblical reference.

    Matthew 1:6

Parenthesis

Parentheses are used to emphasize content. They place more emphasis on the enclosed content than commas. Use parentheses to set off nonessential material, such as dates, clarifying information, or sources, from a sentence.

    Muhammed Ali (1942-present), arguably the greatest athlete of all time, claimed he would "float like a butterfly, sting like a bee."

Dash

Dashes are used to set off or emphasize the content enclosed within dashes or the content that follows a dash. Dashes place more emphasis on this content than parentheses.

    Perhaps one reason why the term has been so problematic—so resistant to definition, and yet so transitory in those definitions—is because of its multitude of applications.

    In terms of public legitimacy—that is, in terms of garnering support from state legislators, parents, donors, and university administrators—English departments are primarily places where advanced literacy is taught.

    The U.S.S. Constitution became known as "Old Ironsides" during the War of 1812—during which the cannonballs fired from the British H.M.S. Guerriere merely bounced off the sides of the Constitution.

    To some of you, my proposals may seem radical—even revolutionary.

Use a dash to set off an appositive phrase that already includes commas. An appositive is a word that adds explanatory or clarifying information to the noun that precedes it.

    The cousins—Tina, Todd, and Sam—arrived at the party together.

The Study Hall Test Preparation Book

Quotation Marks

Use quotation marks to enclose direct quotations.

> He asked, "When will you be arriving?" I answered, "Sometime after 6:30."

Use quotation marks to indicate the novel, ironic, or reserved use of a word.

> History is stained with blood spilled in the name of "justice."

Use quotation marks around the titles of short poems, song titles, short stories, magazine or newspaper articles, essays, speeches, chapter titles, short films, and episodes of television or radio shows.

> "Self-Reliance," by Ralph Waldo Emerson
>
> "Just Like a Woman," by Bob Dylan
>
> "The Smelly Car," an episode of *Seinfeld*

Italics

Underlining and Italics are often used interchangeably. Italicize the titles of magazines, books, newspapers, academic journals, films, television shows, long poems, plays of three or more acts, operas, musical albums, works of art, websites, and individual trains, planes, or ships.

> *Time*
>
> *Romeo and Juliet* by William Shakespeare
>
> *The Metamorphosis of Narcissus* by Salvador Dali
>
> *Amazon.com*
>
> *Titanic*

Italicize foreign words.

> *Semper fi*, the motto of the U.S. Marine Corps, means "always faithful."

Italicize a word or phrase to add emphasis.

> The *truth* is of utmost concern!

Italicize a word when referring to that word.

> The word *justice* is often misunderstood and therefore misused.

The Study Hall Test Preparation Book

Types of Sentences

Independent clause: a clause that has a subject and a verb and can stand alone; a complete sentence

Dependent clause: a clause that has a subject and a verb but cannot stand alone; an incomplete sentence

Simple: composed of 1 independent clause.

Compound: composed of 2 or more independent clauses.

Compound-Complex: composed of 1 or more dependent clauses and 2 or more independent clauses.

The Study Hall Test Preparation Book

Math

The first things we'll cover are **Averages**. The test makers frequently try to confuse you about the number of factors you are dealing with as in this problem:

> John takes a course and is told that two tests and a final will determine his grade. The final will be weighted double. If John has made 86 and 88 on his two tests, what does he have to make on the final to average 90 for the course?

The final is weighted double; so, it has to be represented as a 2x or whatever you want to give as a variable. And the denominator is 4 not 3 because you're weighting that double. But you see how they're trying to disguise what you have to consider. You have to remember that this is weighted double; so, you have to allow for that.

$$\frac{88 + 86 + 2X}{4} = 90$$

This brings up another point about the test. In this case, if you left a 3 in the denominator instead of a 4, trust me, they would have the answer that you come up with as a choice. That is one of the key things about tests. If you work a problem in a wrong direction, they'll have an answer waiting for you every time. So just matching an answer choice is not proof that you have the right.

Let's look at **Percentages**. If I ask you what 1/4% is in decimals, what are you going to tell me? Most people say .25. What you want to remember, and the test maker loves to ask you this because they know with the tic-tic-tic of the clock, you're gonna look at that and say oh, that's .25.

One of the ways they ask this type of question is: 1/4% of 500 = ? You'll go what's .25 of 500? You punch it out on your calculator and come up with 125. But that's wrong!

Remember, if you have the percent sign, or the word percent, you've got to do something with the two decimal places. They are asking for ¼ of 1 percent. It's not even a whole percentage point. This is really: .25% of 500 = .0025 of 500 = 1.25

We're not through with the way they play with percentages yet. You're used to dealing with percentages, as in this problem below:

> The department store wants to decrease the price of a television 25% from its current price of $400.00.

Typically to find out what 25% off is, you take 25% of the price of $400. Then you subtract the resulting $100 from $400. So, you have $300. Unfortunately, this method won't work on the SAT.

There is another way to do it, and that's to do your figuring on the percentage side. We start by saying 100% is the original price. In this case, if I want to take 25% off the price, I'm going to subtract .25 from that 1.00 and have .75. So, I could just multiply that $400 by .75 and get the correct price of $300. This way you're doing your adding and subtracting on the percentage side.

The Study Hall Test Preparation Book

Now, what if I want to increase the price 25%. You add .25 to the 1.00 original price giving you 1.25. So, you multiply by 1.25, and it does the addition for you, giving you the correct answer of $500. Remember, if you are decreasing a price, you multiply by less than 100%. If you are increasing the price, you multiply by a number greater than 100%.

This is where a lot of students say, "Well that's cool, but I'm very comfortable with my old way of doing these problems. Why do I want to fool with doing it a new way?" That's a good question. I have a good answer - the following question:

A car manufacturer increased the price of a car model 30% in 1980 from its original price in 1975. If they increase the price 50% in 1985, how much have they increased the price in the ten years?

(a) 75% (d) 95% (b) 80% (e) 195% (c) 85%

Now, on this problem, a car manufacturer increases the price of a model car 30% in 1980 from its original price in 1975, and in 1985, increased the price 50%. How much did they increase the price over the 10 years? You glance down there, and you look at the answers and say it's got to be 80%. Sorry, that's too easy for a problem in the last few questions, which is where you'd find this one.

This problem illustrates three characteristics of how the test maker treats these problems. The first characteristic is that they didn't give you a starting price...they never do. That doesn't bother us, because we know how to work on the percentage side. What you do is work it like we just did - on the percentage side. You've got 100% to start with as the original price. You're increasing it 30%; so, after adding 30% to the 100% you multiply the original price by 1.30 which gives you 1.30.

This brings us to the second characteristic They want a 50% increase, but you are applying that increase to the new price of 1.30. Increase the price 50%, so you multiply the 1.30 by 1.50 and that leaves you with a total price now of 1.95.

This brings up the third characteristic. Notice that you have (d) as 95% and (e) as 195%. They ask for the total increase. You started with the original price of 1.00. Now we're at 1.95, so the net increase is .95. They ask this question two ways. If they ask it as they have here, how much have they increased the price in 10 years, then the answer is (d). They want to know how much it increased. The other way they ask that question is: "What is the total price after 10 years?" The answer there is, the total price, is 195%. Whether they want the total or they want the increase tells you whether you add or subtract that original 100%.

Now we come to a **Word Problem**. You want to remember that the numbers in a word problem really aren't very difficult. The words are what make word problems difficult. So it makes sense that the way to work word problems is to **get the numbers out of the words**. Think of it this way: If you leave the numbers in the words you are playing their game. If you get the numbers out of the words, you have the ball in your court, so to speak. For example:

The Study Hall Test Preparation Book

Michael made 40% of his first 15 shots. What does he have to average on the rest of his shots if he ends the game with a 50% average of his 30 shots?

You want to get the number out of the words as you read the problem. Michael made 40% of his first 15 shots. What does he have to average on the rest of his shots if he ends the game with a 50% average of his 30 shots? All you see there when you glance at it is shots, shots, shots. In this case, write down what the problem says.

He's made 40% of his first 15 shots. We write down .40 x 15 = 6. So, he's made 6. Where do you want to go? If he wants to make 50% of the 30 shots he takes for the whole game, then we write down .50 x 30 = 15. So what does he have to average?

Well, how many does he have to make to get to 15? 9. How many shots does he have left to do it? 15. So, he's got to make 9 of 15 or 60%. See, once you set that up, that's an easy problem. That's the thing in doing a word problem. Take it apart and do it in components.

They ask two types of **Inequalities**. This first is a "stringout" inequality.

   Solve: $-15 < 3X + 6 < 30$

Your teachers teach you to separate that and work it as two inequalities. I'm going to suggest on the test if you see one of these, leave it as one inequality. It helps keep things simple so you keep uniform in how you work it. Remember that what you do to one segment you do to all three segments.

So in this case you're going to subtract six across because you want to isolate that variable X in the middle. If you subtract six across the board from all of them, you're left with: $-21 < 3X < 24$ Now you divide through by three across the board and are left with: $-7 < X < 8$.

You're going to notice all the way through here we're going to be talking about most frequently is simplifying things. If you see an inequality that you have to solve on these tests your antenna needs to go up and you just need to start searching for a negative that you're going to be multiplying or dividing with because trust me, there will be one there.

   For example : $-5X + 6 < 26$

Subtracting 6 - we have left $-5X < 20$ Then we divide by -5 and, remember when you multiply or divide by a negative number, you reverse the inequality. So we are left with: $X > -4$.

Absolute Values. Nobody has missed this since I started begging. Ergo I'm going to continue begging. When you have an absolute value, perform the operation within the brackets just like it was a parenthesis before you apply that absolute value. So in this case it's $|7+6-18| = |-5| = 5$. It is not applying the absolute value across the board and saying $7+6+18 = 31$. A lot of the things we go over you're going to say: "That looks obvious," but under the pressure of taking the tests in that third hour, you will be surprised some of the stupid things you will do and some of the stupid ways you'll see things.

The Study Hall Test Preparation Book

Exponents. Exponents are fairly straightforward except for a couple of tripping points.

Rule 1: $A^m = A \times A \times A$ "m" times

Number 1 is the easiest in that A to the m is A times itself m number of times.

Rule 2: $A^{-m} = 1/A^m$

Number 2 is where it starts to get a little bit interesting. Number 2 is 1 over A to the m equals A to the negative m.

Rule 3: $A^m + A^n = A^m + A^n$

Number 3 is the most important exponent rule on the test - by far! A to the m plus A to the n equals A to the m plus A to the n. We haven't lost it, this is very important because the test maker will come after you with problems like this (which is very similar to the one everyone missed on the test this one was on.

$X^3 + X^2 = ?$

(A) X^5 (B) X^6 (E) $X^2(X + 1)$

Look at how dastardly they are. You go down here and look at the clue or cues they're giving you, as you glance from the problem to the answer choices, looking at the answers you say: "Oh, I know they think I'm going to multiply these exponents, but I know all you do is add the exponents. So you circle A, go merrily on your way, and never realize you missed it.

Remember!!! If you are adding and subtracting the same number or variable with different exponents, you can't do a thing to the exponents. In the example, all you can do is factor it a bit: $X^2(X + 1)$ You can take X squared out of it so it's X squared times the quantity X plus 1.

Rule 4: $A^m \times A^n = A^{m+n}$

With number 4 you get to do what your impulse was in Number 3. A to the m times A to the n equals A to the m plus n. If you multiply the same number or variable with different exponents, you add the exponents.

Rule 5: $(A^m)^n = A^{mn}$

The only time you multiply exponents is in number 5; when you're raising a power to a power.

Rule 6: $A^m / A^n = A^{m-n}$

Number 6, if you divide, you subtract. A to the M divided by A to the N equals A to the M minus N.

The Study Hall Test Preparation Book

Radicals. Anytime you have a fraction as an exponent you have a radical. For instance: if you've got $A^{1/2}$, that's $\sqrt{A}$. $A^{2/3}$ is $\sqrt[3]{A^2}$.

The $\sqrt{A} \times \sqrt{A} = A$. Just be very careful with that because these tests love, I don't mean likes, I mean love to get rid of a square root that as a clue as to how to work the problem. For instance, the hypotenuse of an isosceles right triangle is side times the square root of 2. They love to give you a side that has square root of 2 in it so when you multiply the square root of two times three times the square root of 2, it comes up with 6. So when you look down to the answers it doesn't give you a clue as to how you got there.

Simultaneous Equations. You know how to do Simultaneous Equations by elimination or by substitution. But on both tests, things are very different. You can't rely on all the methods and techniques from math class. When you see simultaneous equations stacked up or side by side, you must focus on what you are looking for, and then look at what information you haave been given You must focus on the target you are looking forand see how you can use the equations to get there.

For instance, this example:
 If $2x + y = 19$ and $x + 2y = 9$, then what is the value of $3x + 3y$?
 a) 9
 b) 10
 c) 19
 d) 28
 e) It cannot be determined from the information given.

So they give you $x + 2y = 19$, $2x + y = 9$. Under those conditions, what is the value of $3x + 3y$?. If you try to solve for x and y you'll fill up a page and, at the least, get tough fractions to work with. For some reason it just doesn't mix right. You must focus on the target - on $3x + 3y$! Then look at $2x + y = 19$ and $x + 2y = 9$ and see how you can manipulate those equations to get to your target. So if you add the two equations you find that $2x + y = 19$ plus $x + 2y = 9$ equals
$3x + 3y = 28$. SO the value of $3x + 3y$ is 28!

This won't help you solve for x and y at all, but it will help you get the answer for the test. Just add the two equations together, and remember that technique because it shows up often. You may have to add the equations, subtract them, or manipulate them in a manner which will get you to your target. Just remember to manipulate the equations in whatever manner you have to in order to get to your target.

The Study Hall Test Preparation Book

Simultaneous Equations in Word Problems.

   Alex is twice as old as Connie. Connie is two years younger than Janice. If their average age is 22, how old is Connie?

The majority of simultaneous equations that they ask you to solve are going to be in the form of a word problem like this. What you do with the word problem, as we said before, is get the numbers out of the words. In this case, identify who or what you're looking for, put everything else in terms of that, and then solve the problem.
In this problem, who are we looking for here? We're looking for Connie. So, put everybody in Connie's terms. Alex is twice as old as Connie which we denote with 2C. Connie is two years younger than Janice, so we denote that with C + 2. If their average age is 22, how old is Connie? So you set up your equation:

$$\frac{A + C + J}{3} = 22$$

Now you substitute and get 2C + 2 + C + C = 66; 4C = 64; Connie is 16. So just identify who you're looking for, put the others in terms of that character or that individual, boom you've got the answer. They aren't difficult, it's just a question of having a technique for doing it.

Scientific Notation. This shouldn't be a problem for you since you can use your calculator. Just remember:
$4 \times 10^5 = 400,000$; $7 \times 10^4 = 70,000$. You just count the number of zeros to the right of the number.

There is one particular situation pertaining to scientific notation which the test seems to enjoy presenting. This is where they ask you to multiply two numbers written in scientific notation. Separate the numbers and the powers ot ten. Multiply the numbers and treat the powers of ten the same as you would any other number multiplied by itself with different exponents. For example:
$(4 \times 10^6)(7 \times 10^7) = (4 \times 7)(10^{13}) = 28 \times 10^{13} = 2.8 \times 10^{14}$

Again, the technique to remember is to separate and treat them separately. So you take 4 and 7 and multiply those together and multiply the result of that by, (just treat 10 as you would any other number with an exponent) 5 plus 6, equals 28 times 10 to the 11th. Remember with Scientific Notation, you have to reduce the number you raising to the power of ten to a single decimal point.

The Study Hall Test Preparation Book

Supplementary Angles share a line and total 180 degrees.

Intersecting lines form **Vertical Angles** and opposite vertical are equal.

Area
The area of a **square** is side squared: s^2.

The area of a **rectangle** is length times width: L x W.

The area of a **circle** is πr² where r is the radius
The circumference of a circle is 2πr where r is the radius or π times diameter.

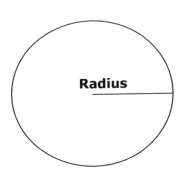

The area of a triangle is 1/2 of the product of the base and height. (base x height)/2 And they don't give it to you in a straightforward fashion. Rather they use figures like this one.

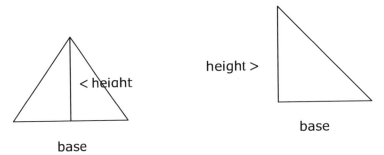

Remember that any side of a triangle can be the base of a triangle as long as you can determine the perpendicular distance from the base to the opposite angle

The Study Hall Test Preparation Book

Volume

If you've got a solid rectangle, it's (length x width x height).

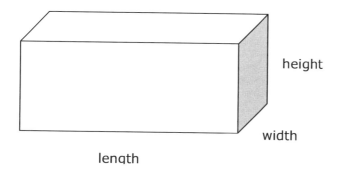

A solid cube is just side cubed.

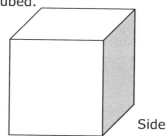

A cylinder is the area of the circle, πr² multiplied by the height.

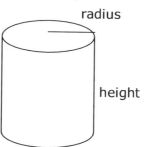

The Study Hall Test Preparation Book

The **Pythagorean Theorem** is all over the test. $a^2 + b^2 = c^2$, where a & b are the two sides of a right triangle and c is the hypotenuse.

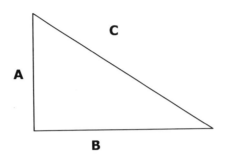

Special Triangles
Because it is so common, there's three shortcuts to it that will help because there are three very repeatable and very particular types of triangles that show up on the test. One of them is a 30-60 right triangle. So it's angles are 30-60. The short side opposite the 30 is S. The longer side is S√3. And the hypotenuse is 2S. Remember it as S times √3 because 30 starts with a three and 2S because 60 is twice 30.

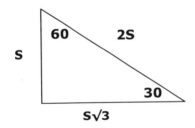

studyhalldallas.com

The Study Hall Test Preparation Book

The next one is a triplet, and this is a triplet that shows up all over the tests. It's a 3, 4, 5 right triangle or 6, 8, 10. It's just that ratio that exists.

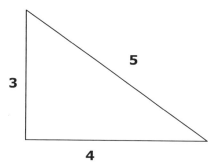

The last triangle is the 45-45. The formula for the area of this, incidentally, is side squared divided by 2. The formula for the hypotenuse is side (S)√2. Remember the square root of two because you have two equal sides to the triangle.

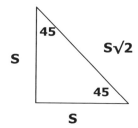

With regard to **Congruent triangles**, they are not going to come out and blatantly say that these triangles are congruent. They will give you information like side-angle-side, angle-side-angle, or side-side-side that says you can determine if they are congruent.

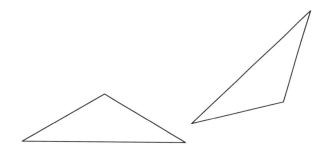

The Study Hall Test Preparation Book

Similar triangles have the same angles. They have proportionate sides, but they are not identical. Triangles A and B are proportionate because they have equal angles. Notice that, if the line in triangle C is parallel to the base, it creates 2 similar triangles.

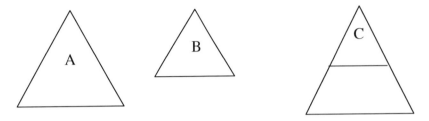

Functions A function is an equation written to determine coordinate values. You must be disciplined and make the substitutions indicated. For instance:

$$f(x) = x^2 - 6x + 10 \qquad g(x) = x + 2$$

$$f(2) = ? \qquad f(g(2)) = ? \qquad f(g(x)) = ?$$

If you are asked what is f(2), you take 2 and substitute it in for x. If I ask you for f(g(2)), you take that 2 and plug it in the g(x) function, take that resulting 4 and substitute it for x in the f(x) function. If I ask you what is f(g(x)), you look carefully and see that all you have been given for g(x) is x + 2. You are simply substituting.

Remember with **Graphs**, they are down to linear distance. So, if they say: "What is the distance from -2 to 7?" The answer is 9. Distance is distance whether it is positive or negative.

More Averages When you add or subtract a value equal to the average, there is no change in the average.

Sigmund, Ingrid, Siegfried, and Gunther average age is 67. Gunther is 67 when he dies. What is the average age of the three who remain?

Remember, if you add or subtract a number equal to the average to the average, it has no impact on the average. So, if you've got one like Sigrid, Sigfried, and Gunther averaging age 67. Gunther is 67 when he moves, what is the average age of those who remain? The answer is 67. The average doesn't change.

They have another way of asking it. They say Sally has played five rounds of golf, and her average score is 75. She plays a sixth round, and her score is 75. What's the average now? 75, it just doesn't change.

studyhalldallas.com

The Study Hall Test Preparation Book

This next one is crucial. They have been asking **change in average** problems very frequently recently. For instance:

> Al, Bubba, and Sally have an average age of 17. Mary Jo joins their group and the average age becomes 22. How old is Mary Jo?

This is a very typical change in average problem. Now, you are smart enough to set-up an equation to figure this out, but there is a much easier way to do it. Go out where the question is vulnerable - to the totals. If there are three of them and the average age is 17, they have 51 years. If there are four of them and their average age is 22, they have 88 years. Somebody brought 37 years to the party. It makes a difference there, and that's Mary Jo. If you simply go out to the totals, the answer is just really easy to come by. Remember in averages, you are just talking totals of something and the number of factors that go into that total.

Proportions These are just ratio problems where you set up two ratios and solve for the missing part. For example:

> A recipe for 60 cookies uses 3 cups of flour. How many cups of flour will be needed to make 150 cookies?

When you can, set proportion problems up as ratio as in this case: $60/3 = 150/X$. By setting this problem up as a ratio, you can solve it by cross multiplying and it allows you to be able to check to make certain your ratio is set up to compare like entities.

If you are told that something is the ratio of 1 to 3 realize what that's really saying. If I say that the ratio of boys to girls is 1 to 3, then what I'm meaning is that 1/4 of the students are boys and 3/4 are girls. That is a ratio of 1 part to 3 parts.

Another type of **Ratio** problem is an expanding ratio problem. For example:

> A high school has 700 students. The ratio of freshmen to sophomores to juniors to seniors is 4:3:2:1. How many juniors are there?

This second one is easy math. The high school has 700 students. They are in a ratio of freshmen to sophomores to juniors to seniors of 4 to 3 to 2 to 1. So, you need to determine the factor that will expand this ratio to the correct total.
$4X+3X+2X+1X =700$. So, 700 students equals 10X. Dividing through by 10 gives you X equaling 70.
The answer to this, answer a, they'll give you 70. This is a two step problem. You've got to go back and plug it in and be sure you plug it in the right one. People first of all say "Yes, I've got an answer to this thing," and take 70, and are so relieved to get an answer. And they don't know they missed the problem. Or they go back up and, because we all think of seniors as 4 and juniors as 3. They go back and fit it into 3x. It's not 3x, it's 2x because they want the number of juniors. Be certain to reread the problem to see where it fits.

The Study Hall Test Preparation Book

Work Problems The key to work problems is to figure out where you link the two - what you're going to deal with that's common between the two workers. These relate to different people working at different rates. There are two variations on this problem: Independent work and Teamwork.

Independent Work 1. Find out work completed for each for same duration. 2. Multiply first workers rate by time he works. 3. Find portion of work remaining. 4. Multiply by second worker. Example:

> Lin can mow the lawn in 3 hours. Charles can mow it in 4 hours. If Lin mows for 2 hours and C finishes the job, how long will it take Charles?

On this first one, Lin can mow the lawn in 3 hours, Charles can mow it in 4 hours. If Lin's mowed for 2 hours, how long will it take Charles to finish the job?

Where you are unifying them or uniting them is that there is one piece of work here, one job. Lin's mowed for two hours, and he does 1/3 in an hour. If he has worked for 2 hours, he has done 2/3 of this yard. So, there's 1/3 of this job left, and how long does it take Charles to do that whole job, 4 hours. So, 1/3 of 4 is 4/3. So, it's going to take Charles 1 and 1/3 hours to finish it. Easy.

Teamwork 1. Find portion each worker completes for same duration. 2. Add rates together to find portion they can complete together. 3. Divide total job by combined rate to find length of time. Example:

> Lin can mow the lawn in 3 hours. Charles can mow it in 4 hours. Working together, how long will it take?

On this next one, you are dealing with teamwork. So, you are unifying them in terms of their work rate. Lin mows the lawn in 3 hours. Charles mows it in 4 hours. Therefore, what is Lin mowing per hour? 1/3 per hour. What is Charles mowing per hour? 1/4 per hour. Together they mow 7/12 of the yard per hour. So, it has taken them 1 hour to do it and they've got 5/12 left. They've got 5/12 left.

There's two ways to figure this answer. One is to look at the answers that they give you. Right now, they are probably going to give you 1 hour, 1 and 1/4, 1 and 1/2, 1 and 3/4, and 2 hours. It's more than 1 hour. If this was 3.5/12, that would be 1 and ½ hours, but it's more than that. So, it's more than those and it's not 2 hours; so, it's gotta be 1 and 3/4 hours. What people do is unfortunately go over and they multiply 5/12 by 60. The other way to do this is to set up a ratio. 7 is to 5 as 60 is to x. You solve for that, you find out that the x is 43. So there are two ways to do that problem, but the main thing is the way you set it up.

The Study Hall Test Preparation Book

People moving problems People have an undue amount of trouble with these. The key to doing a people-moving problem is to draw it out or write it out, so you can see what is really going on with the problem.

Example: Joan left in her car driving 50 miles per hour three hours ago. If Ellen leaves now driving 60 miles per hour and neither one of the girls stop or slow down, how long will it take Ellen to catch Joan?

Joan left driving her car 3 hours ago going 50 miles per hour. Ellen leaves right now driving 60 miles per hour. How long would it take her to catch Joan if neither one of them stops or slows down? Write down what it says. Joan left going 50 miles per hour 3 hours ago. How far is she ahead? 150 miles. Ellen's driving 60 miles per hour. So, she's driving 10 miles per hour faster. So, she's catching up at 10 miles per hour. She'll catch up in 15 hours. See how easy it is once you write it out and conceptualize it. That's all you do with these people-moving problems. Make them make sense so you can see the actual problem, and then nail it.

Absolutely remember that the exterior angle of a triangle equals the sum of the two non-adjacent interior angles. They will turn this triangle upside down and sideways, but the question they ask is the same. So, $k = a + b$.

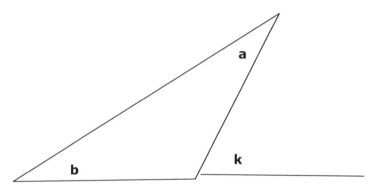

When a test asks questions about the size of the sides of a triangle, the central question is whether or not you recall that the sum of any 2 sides of a triangle exceeds the 3rd side. For example:

If the lengths of the sides of a triangle are 7, 2x, and x, which of the following is a possible value of x?

(A) 1 (B) 2 (C) 4 (D) 7 (E) 8

This is easy, once you know what they are asking for. Just add two sides - any two sides together. So: $7 + 2x > x$ and, subtracting x from both sides, you are left with $7 > x$. The take two other sides: $x + 2x > 7$. $3x > 7$ and, dividing through by 3, you find $x > 4/3$. Looking at the answer choices, you are left with only 4 as a possible choice.

The Study Hall Test Preparation Book

Please remember the **Surface area** of a cube is the areas of six faces and not eight. I know that you wouldn't have made that error, but some people have.

The **Loaf problem**. If I give you a loaf of bread, and I say I want 6 pieces out of that loaf and I want to use the whole loaf. How many cuts do I make? Five, exactly. Because that last one is already made. You want the total pieces you want minus one. Just remember that t minus 1. They ask a lot of questions that have to do with that. It may be cutting pieces of brick or etc.

That little t minus 1 comes in very handy. They may say I am putting up barbed wire, and I am putting 4 feet of barbed wire between each fence post. If I say that I have 16 fence posts, how much barbed wire have I laid? Most people say 16 times 4. It's 15 times 4 because the first post doesn't generate distance.

With regard to **Statistics**, The MEAN is the average. The MEDIAN is the 50th percentile. The MODE is the most frequent score.

$$90 - 3$$
$$85 - 1$$
$$80 - 1$$
$$75 - 2$$
$$70 - 1$$
$$65 - 1$$

If someone gave a test and the students score as shown on the chart above, the Mean would be the arithmetic average, the Median would be 80, because 4 students scored above 80 and 4 students scored below 80, and the mode is 90 because the most common score on the test was 90.

Order of operations Remember to: 1. Evaluate all powers 2. Do all multiplications and divisions from left to right 3. Do all additions and subtractions from left to right. PEMDAS is the acronym which you can remember as "Please Excuse My Dear Aunt Sally."

The Study Hall Test Preparation Book

Probability. Probability is simply the number of possible outcomes divided by the number of desired or looked for outcomes. Two examples follow:

> You have 8 blue shirts, 6 red shirts, and 4 white shirts. After you take a blue shirt out, what's the probability you will take a blue shirt out again.

The key here is to remember to subtract from your total. In this case, we have 7 blue shirts left and a total of 17 shirts in the closet. So you have a 7 in 17 chance of pulling out a blue shirt.

Another, more difficult, problem would involve multiple variables For instance:

> You have two dice, each numbered from 1 - 6. What is the probability that you will roll a combination That totals 7?

When you look at this analytically, you could have a 1 and a 6, 6 and 1, 2 and 5, 5 and 2, 3 and 4, and 4 and 3 which is 6 combinations that work. How many total combinations are possible? If you roll a 1 on one cube, how many other possible numbers can come up on the other cube? Six! So, you have six combinations of six each - or 36 total combinations. So the answer we're looking for is 6/36 or 1/6..

X & Y Intercepts

Periodically on the test you will need to determine the X or the Y intercept. To do so, simply set either X or Y equal to 0. If you set X equal to 0, then you'll be able to determine the X intercept point because that's where the line will cross the X axis.

Abstractions

Frequently the question will be too abstract for you to be able to arrive at an answer easily. In these cases you can do one of two things depending on the nature the question. You can plug in the values that you determine as in this problem:

> A drill bit used by an oil drilling company will last for n feet. If each hole is q feet deep, how many drill bits are needed for x holes.

To solve this problem, give the variables values. Let's say that a drill bit lasts 100 feet. Each hole has to be 300 feet deep. If they want to drill 4 wells then you simply work it thusly.

$$\frac{300 \text{ ft}}{100}(4) = 12 \quad \text{so substitute the letters} \quad \frac{qx}{n}$$

Or you can plug in the answer choices to see which one works. This is important -- plug in answer choices starting with the last answer choice and working your way to the first answer choice because frequently the test makers like to make you work through several incorrect answers to take more of your time.

The Study Hall Test Preparation Book

If you are told that something is the **ratio** of 1 to 3 realize what that's really saying. If I say that the ratio of boys to girls is 1 to 3, then what I'm meaning is that 1/4 of the students are boys and 3/4 are girls. That is a ratio of 1 part to 3 parts.

Whenever you see a **Split Numerator in a Fraction**, as in this problem:

$$\frac{R+N}{R}$$

Remember you always split the numerator and apply the denominator to each number, giving yourself two fractions. This doesn't work sometimes on the tests, it works all of the time. So:

$$\frac{R+N}{R} = \frac{R}{R} + \frac{N}{R} = 1 + \frac{N}{R}$$

Remember that's they love to slide multiple concepts into math problems. By that we mean there will be one or more sides or facets to a problem as they try to measure more than one math principal.

If they ask about the number of students in classes remember that you have to discount the **Overlapping** students. As in this problem:

> There are 78 students taking math class. There are 102 students enrolled in science 46 students take science and math. How many students are attending the two classes?

> You simply add the two classes 78 + 102 = 180, then you subtract the students that OVERLAP. So 180 - 46 = 134 actual students.

When you see **shaded regions** on the test you'll be subtracting one geometric form from another to determine the shaded area. Therefore the steps are to focus on the stated regions to identify the types of geometric forms you are looking at, determining the areas of the appropriate regions, and subtract one from another.

The Study Hall Test Preparation Book

If they give you **Fractions within Fractions**, remember the two rules that apply. If they give you a fraction in the numerator remember that it drops down, in effect, and you multiply the two denominators together as in this problem.

$$\frac{\frac{1}{4}}{3} = \frac{1}{4 \times 3} = \frac{1}{12}$$

If they give you a fraction in the denominator remember that you have to flip it so that you are multiplying the numerator by the reciprocal of the denominator. As in this problem:

$$\frac{3}{\frac{1}{4}} = \frac{3 \times 4}{1} = 12$$

Also remember that if you're estimating problems and are looking at gallons of something, when you get a fraction of a gallon, it rounds up to the next whole gallon. As in this problem:

> If it takes 2 gallons to paint eight square feet of wall, how many gallons are needed to paint four walls, each wall measuring 11 x 9?

You would first multiply 11 and 9 to get 99. Then multiply the per wall area by 4 because you have 4 walls and get 396, which you divide by 8 to see how many 8s there are in 396. You get 49.5, so you need 50 gallons of paint.

Note that this type of estimating problem can also be done using hours or parts of hours for a price per hour.

You can be sure to see at least one **Remainder** problem because they have realized that students today are quite dependent on their calculators. They will offer problems that take the calculator out of your hands. The two most common types of remainder problems follow.

They may propose a question where you have to do something with the remainder.

> The school had a shortage of teachers and needed to decrease the number of classes from 28 to 25. If the each of the 28 classes has 22 students and the students are distributed evenly amongst the new classes, how many classes will have an extra student.

All you have to do here is find your total number of students and divide by 25. Remember that there is a real number of students left over, so either do the division by hand or use the calculator correctly.

By hand: 28 x 22 = 616
616 ÷ 25 = [24 x 25 = 600] 24 classes with <u>16</u> students left since
616 − 600 = 16

The Study Hall Test Preparation Book

By calculator: 28 x 22 = 616
616 ÷ 25 = 24.64
.64 x 25 = 16

Or they may ask you a question where they want you to determine remainders without giving you specific numbers.

If the remainder when x is divided by 5 is 2, what is the reminder when 3x is divided by 5?

Simply pick a number that make the first part of the statement true. Let's say 7 (or 12, or 22, or 17) in this case.
7 x 3 = 21 (12 x 3 = 36) (22 x 3 = 66) (17 x 3 = 51)
ALL have a remainder of 1 when divided by 5

Two types of **Sequence** problems can show up. The sequence can follow a pattern, like:
4,7,10, 13……..
where you are simply adding 3 to the term before it. You would determine the nth term by using the formula: 4 (the first term in the sequence) = 3 (n – 1). You use n – 1 so you don't count the first term which is 4. So this problem might be:

Find the 23rd term in the sequence: 4,7,10,13……..

4 + 3(23 – 1) = 4 + 3(22) = 4 + 66 = 70

You may also see sequences which involve geometric or exponential growth. This is a sequence which involves a ratio between consecutive terms. You might find this in a population type problem (the population doubles every 4 years) or one like this:

In the sequence 3, 12, 48, 192………. what would be the 8th term?

First we determine the ratio: 12 ÷ 3 = 4: 48 ÷ 12 = 4: 192 ÷ 48 = 4 so our ratio is 4. 3 is the first term so our equation is: $3 \times 4^{n-1} = 3 \times 4^{8-1} = 3 \times 4^7 = 3 \times 16{,}384 = 49{,}152$ (They will usually involve smaller numbers.)

Direct and Inverse Variation problems address how numbers vary. Numbers vary **directly** if there is a common factor, ie: y and x vary directly if y = kx where k is a constant and y/x = k.
For example: y = 4x and then:
y = 8…….x = 2
y = 12….x = 5
y = 32….x = 8

If y and x vary **inversely** the product of the two variables is a constant. Therefore y = k/x.
For example: y = 30/x and then:
y = 3…….x = 10
y = 6…….x = 5
y = 10…..x = 3

studyhalldallas.com

The Study Hall Test Preparation Book

There are problems that can be solved using **Trigonometry**. So far it appears that these will be relatively simple instances of **Special Triangles** (30/60, 45/45, or 3-4-5 right triangles).

Remembering **SOHCAHTOA** should be sufficient for solving these problems if you prefer using trigonometry over geometry. The acronym applies to the assignment of values below. The acronym is useful for determining the values of the sine, cosine, and tangents of angles.

Sin A = $\frac{\text{opposite}}{\text{hypotenuse}}$

Cos A = $\frac{\text{adjacent}}{\text{hypotenuse}}$

Tan A = $\frac{\text{opposite}}{\text{adjacent}}$

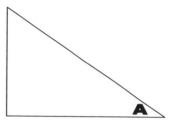

When you encounter **Slope** problems, remember that slope is "Rise over run," or, in other words, the change in the "y" value divided by the change in the "x" value on an xy coordinate graph. (Special note: horizontal lines have a slope of "0," vertical lines have undefined slopes, parallel lines have the same slope, and perpendicular lines have negative reciprocal slopes [their product is -1]).

A **Permutation** is when the number of choices will be affected by previous choices. For instance:
> You are asked to assign a number to 5 different desks. You can use any one of the digits 1-9, but you can't repeat any of them. How many combinations are possible?

You have 9 possible digits to use for the first desk. Once you've used that number you can't repeat it, so you only have 8 numbers to select from now. Since you will have used 2 numbers now, you have 7 choices for the third desk.
> So, to work it out: 9 x 8 x 7 x 6 x 5 = 15,120 possibilities.

If the order in which the numbers are chosen makes no difference then it's termed a **Combination**. If it's a completely random combination you can solve it using the number of items factorial. For example:
> When the student council was deciding on the order the 5 bands would appear in the "Battle of the Bands" they had how many possible combinations to choose from?

You have 5 bands involved and the order is random so you can use the factorial of 5.
> 5! = 5 x 4 x 3 x 2 x 1 = 120

studyhalldallas.com

The Study Hall Test Preparation Book

Radians
A radian is the ratio between the length of an arc in a circle and the circle's radius.
1 radian = 180/Π degrees so when you convert radians to degrees, multiply by 180/Π.

1 Radian = Π = 180
2 Π = 360
Π/2 = 90
3 Π/2 = 270

Circle Graph Equation

The equation for a circle is (x – "x value at center")² + (y – "y value at the center")² = radius²

So, if we have a circle with a center at (3,4) and a radius of 5, the equation would be:
(x – 3)² + (y – 4)² = 5²

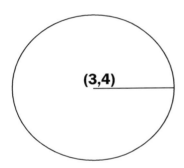

Logarithms
The **logarithm** of a number is the <u>exponent</u> by which another fixed value, the <u>base</u>, has to be raised to produce that number.

$\log_a(b)$ = c where a is the base or number, b is the outcome when a is raised to the exponential power c.
For example:
    $\log_2(8)$ = 3
    2^3 = 8

Matrices
Don't panic when you see a matrix on the tests. They use them simply to organize numbers or letters into columns and rows. You will see something like this:

[5 3 1]
[4 2 7]
[0 6 5]

You will be presented with questions about rows or columns or patterns displayed in the matrix

The Study Hall Test Preparation Book

Distance Rate Formula
Familiarize yourself with the distance rate formula which states that **distance = rate x time**.

Remember the easy formula where if you go 100 miles driving 50 mph it will take you 2 hours.
100mi/50mph = 2 hr

If you keep this formula in mind, you can use it to identify the relationship and identify the missing element.

Trigonometry

Other than remembering **SOHCAHTOA** you may need to know the reciprocals of sine, cosine, and tangent: cosecant, secant, and cotangent.

cosecant A = 1/sinA

secant A = 1/cosA

cotangent A = 1/tanA

Domain and Range
$\quad$ f(x) = y

domain = all the "x" values that can go into the function
range = all the "y" values that can be created
The above list of points, being a relationship between certain *x*'s and certain *y*'s, is a relation. The domain is all the *x*-values, and the range is all the *y*-values. To give the domain and the range, I just list the values without duplication:

Imaginary Numbers
$\sqrt{-1}$ is impossible, so imaginary number "i" is used.
For example:
$\sqrt{-16} = \sqrt{4}\sqrt{-1} = 4i$
and:
$i^0 = 1$
$i^1 = i$
$i^2 = -1 \quad \{(\sqrt{-1})^2 = -1\}$
$i^3 = (i^2)(i^1) = (-1)(i) = -i$
$i^4 = (i^2)(i^2) = (-1)(-1) = 1$
then the sequence repeats

The Study Hall Test Preparation Book

Complex Numbers
Complex numbers are composed of a real number and an imaginary number
5 + 3i
real – imaginary

when you add and subtract, you add and subtract like terms
(3 + 2i) + (-1 + i) =
(3+-1) + (2i + i) =
2 + 3i

when you multiply, you FOIL
(5 + 2i)(4 – 3i) =
$20 - 15i + 8i - 6i^2$ =
20 – 7i + 6 =
26 – 7i

When you divide, you cannot have i in the denominator

$$\frac{4 + 2i}{3 - i}$$

$$\frac{4 + 2i}{3 - i} * \frac{3 + i}{3 + i} =$$

$$\frac{12 + 4i + 6i + 2i^2}{9 + 3i - 3i - i^2} =$$

$$\frac{12 + 10i - 2}{9 + 1} =$$

$$\frac{10 + 10i}{10} =$$

1 + i

Trigonometric Identities
In mathematics, an "identity" is an equation which is always true. These can be "trivially" true, like "$x = x$" or usefully true, such as the Pythagorean Theorem's "$a^2 + b^2 = c^2$" for right triangles. There are loads of trigonometric identities, but the following are the ones you're most likely to see and use.

$sin^2 + cos^2 = 1$

tan = sin/cos

cosØ = sin(90 - Ø)
sinØ = cos(90 - Ø)

Periods:

Let's start with the basic sine function, $f(t) = sin(t)$. This function has an amplitude of 1 because the graph goes one unit up and one unit down from the midline of the graph. This function has a period of 2π because the sine wave repeats every 2π units. The graph looks like this:

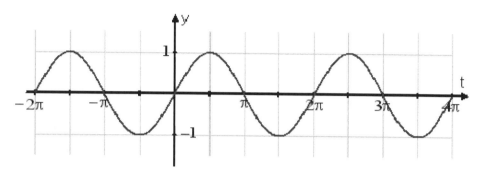

sin and cos have period of 2Π
    tan has period of Π

The Study Hall Test Preparation Book

The Study Hall Test Preparation Book

ACT Preparation

There are several characteristics of the ACT.

First, you **answer every question** on the test to the point of guessing. There is no "penalty" for guessing, so answer everything.

Secondly, you **must account for the time** on the test as a great deal of the difficulty is derived from the fact that the test imposes severe time constraints. When practicing the tests you must work on your speed and be careful not to get "stuck" on questions. You can see the time constraints when you look at the structure of the test.

If you run out of time, choose the question column that you haven't filled out in a while and choose that location for the rest of your answers.

ACT Structure

English Test	75 ques	45 min
Math Test	60 ques	60 min
Reading Test	40 ques	35 min
Science Test	40 ques	35 min

English Test

Content/skills	Percent	Questions
Usage/mechanics	53%	**40**
Punctuation	13%	10
Grammar and usage	16%	12
Sentence structure	24%	18
Rhetorical skills	47%	35
Strategy	16%	12
Organization	15%	11
Style	16%	12

Mathematics Test

Content	Percent	Questions
Pre-algebra	23%	14
Elementary algebra	17%	10
Intermediate algebra	15%	9
Coordinate geometry	15%	9
Plane geometry	23%	14
Trigonometry	7%	4

The Study Hall Test Preparation Book

Reading Test

Content	Percent	Questions
Humanities	25%	10
Prose fiction	25%	10
Social studies	25%	10
Natural sciences	25%	10

Science Test

Scientific content can be from Biology, Chemistry, Physics, or Earth/Space sciences.

The content is presented using different data formats in such a way that uses passages, graphs, charts, tables, and experimental visual representations. Questions are applied to the content area.

Format	Percent	Questions
Data representation	38%	15
Research summaries	45%	18
Conflicting viewpoints	17%	7

The Study Hall Test Preparation Book

ACT English Usage

Content/skills	Percent	Questions
Usage/mechanics	**53%**	**40**
Punctuation	13%	10
Grammar and usage	16%	12
Sentence structure	24%	18

The Punctuation questions deal with correct use of commas, semi-colons, colons, and general punctuation.

The Grammar and usage questions concern the correct placement and usage of words.

The Sentence structure questions will question the mechanics of sentences and correct placement of words.

Content/skills	Percent	Questions
Rhetorical skills	**47%**	**35**
Strategy	16%	12
Organization	15%	11
Style	16%	12

The Strategy questions apply to the appropriateness of sentences and phrasing.

The Organization questions are about the order and coherence of the passage.

The Style questions will address effective word choice and sentence usage.

The Study Hall Test Preparation Book

ACT Science

Science covered:
    Biology
    Chemistry
    Earth/Space Science
    Physics

You really don't need advanced subject knowledge, rather all you need is some knowledge of terms, concepts, and procedures. Basically you need to be familiar with scientific reasoning. You may need minimal math skills.

Formats
There are three formats for presenting the questions and problems.

Data Representation
Research Format
Conflicting Viewpoints

They proportions of the test for each format is approximately:

Data Representation	15 questions	38%
Research Summaries	18 questions	45%
Conflicting Viewpoints	7 questions	17%

Data Representation
    These questions will be asking you to interpret charts, graphs, diagrams, and experimental data. You may be asked to:
- form reasonable hypotheses or inferences
- identify variables and variable relationships
- coordinate graphs and related keys
- interpret axis labels and relationship with data points
- relate new data or data empirical information

Research Summaries
    These questions will be regarding descriptions of related experiments or studies. These may be about the results, designs, and techniques of experiments or studies. You may be asked to:
- form reasonable hypotheses or inferences
- identify similarities and differences
- identify variables and controls
- analyze experimental design and strengths and weaknesses
- recognize assumptions and hypotheses

The Study Hall Test Preparation Book

Conflicting Viewpoints

These will be questions about views or interpretations of the same data or phenomenon that differ. You may be asked to:
- identify the conflicting elements of the views
- determine similarities and differences
- determine alternate viewpoints

You will need to keep several considerations in mind as you evaluate the various charts, graphs, and data presentations you will encounter.

This is a typical data representation question:

Passage I

Figure 1 depicts some of the steps of protein synthesis in eukaryotes.

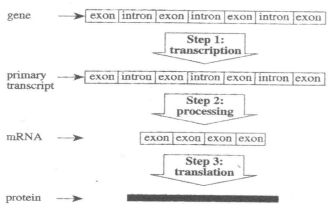

Figure 1

In yeast, the genes that are expressed at a given time depend on environmental conditions, such as the glucose concentration in the environment.

Saccharomyces cerevisiae, a type of yeast, was grown for 12 hours on a growth medium containing glucose. The transcription rates of 4 genes (Genes 1–4) were determined. The *relative transcription rate* (RTR) of each gene was then calculated using the following formula:

$$RTR = \frac{\text{the gene's transcription rate at a given time}}{\text{the gene's transcription rate at time} = 0 \text{ hr}}$$

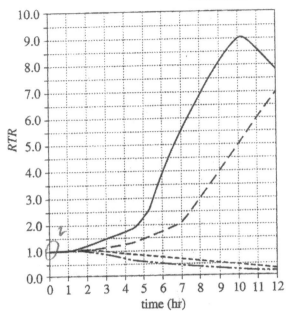

Figure 2

It would contain several figures:

Figure 3 shows the glucose concentration of the medium during the experiment.

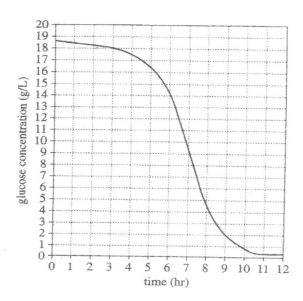

Figure 3

Figures 2 and 3 adapted from Joseph L. DeRisi, Vishwanath R. Iyer, and Patrick O. Brown, "Exploring the Metabolic and Genetic Control of Gene Expression on a Genomic Scale." ©1997 by the American Association for the Advancement of Science.

And questions:

1. At which of the following times was the transcription rate of Gene 2 the greatest?

    A. Time = 0 hr
    B. Time = 2 hr
    C. Time = 4 hr
    D. Time = 6 hr

2. At which of the following times was the transcription rate of Gene 2 closest to 2 times the transcription rate of Gene 2 at time = 0 hr ?

    F. Time = 5 hr
    G. Time = 7 hr
    H. Time = 9 hr
    J. Time = 10 hr

3. Which of the following cellular components is most directly involved in Step 3 in Figure 1 ?

    A. Cell membrane
    B. Chloroplasts
    C. Lysosomes
    D. Ribosomes

4. Based on Figure 1, which of the following best describes what happens to introns during gene expression?

    F. Introns are transcribed and then translated.
    G. Introns are translated and then transcribed.
    H. Introns are transcribed, but not translated.
    J. Introns are translated, but not transcribed.

5. According to Figures 2 and 3, when the glucose concentration of the medium was 12 g/L, the *RTR* of Gene 4 was closest to which of the following?

    A. 0.1
    B. 0.5
    C. 0.9
    D. 1.3

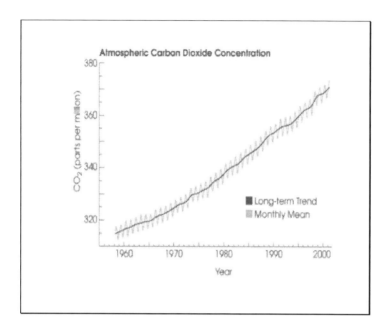

One of the first things you must attend to is identifying what is being measured and portrayed. Look closely at the axes and look for trends in the data portrayed. Here we are at carbon dioxide concentration over a period of years.

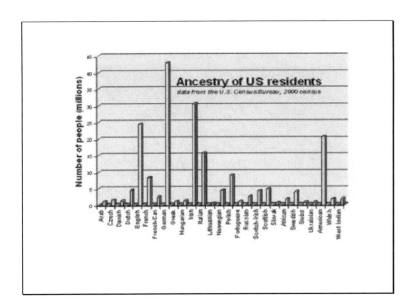

You may encounter two related graphs and be asked to determine why they may differ.

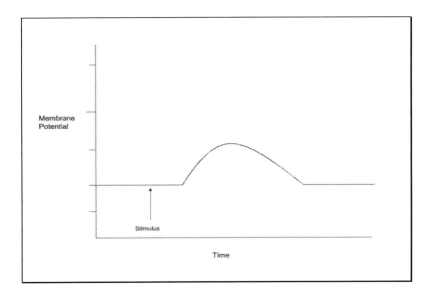

In this case we see there is a latency after a stimulus is applied before there is an increase in membrane potential. You would be expected to derive an opinion from information on the graph and the information accompanying the graphs.

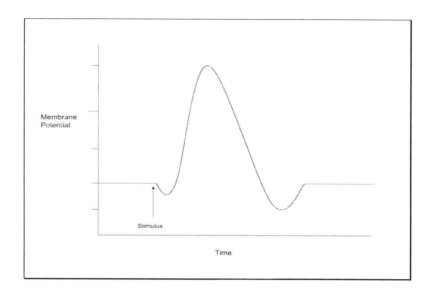

In this case there is no latency and there is a decrease before there is a spike in the membrane potential. You would identify reasons for the different reaction from the experimental data and information.

Food	Mass(g)	Change in Temp	Heat Released
Ham	2.0	28.3	31.4
Tomato	2.0	4.6	6.5
Avocado	2.0	21.4	24.9
Bread	2.0	14.9	16.2

You might be given a chart where you must identify similar trends and generalities. You may also be asked to identify differences.

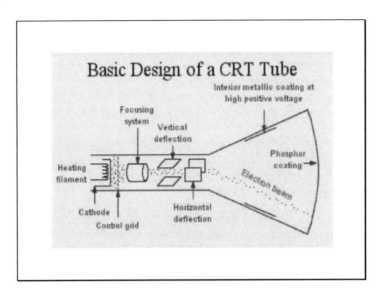

You may be asked to provide a reason from an experiment for a change made apparent in the diagram.

Variables

Some of the most important elements of experiments and experimental design are variables. There are several types of variables and manipulating them makes for effective design. Let's look at an experiment and the role variables play in the experiement.

Does an electric fan turn faster if the voltage tuning the fan is increased?

We must measure the **amount of voltage**..........................The **Independent Variable**

We observe and measure the **number of revolutions** ....The **Dependent Variable**

We use the **same motor**..The **Controlled Variable**

The Study Hall Test Preparation Book

The SAT Test

The SAT is not an intelligence test. It's not a test of how smart you are. It's not a test of how well educated you are. It's a test of how well you can take the SAT. For me to say you can get 200 points smarter in here is a preposterous statement. To say you can get 200 points better on the SAT is a very real possibility. That statement, in and of itself, goes to show that the SAT is not a test of intelligence; it's a test of how well you take the SAT. So we can accept that it's not a good test. But it's what's being used by the colleges. The rules that are established by colleges for admittance are that the SAT is one of the criteria for getting in. So it is a tool you can use; and I'd look at it that way.

SAT STUCTURE

Structure and Time Allotments.

Math	63 Questions	80 Minutes
Reading	52 Questions	65 Minutes
Writing	44 Questions	35 Minutes
Essay (optional)		50 Minutes

More specifically:

Section 1 – 65 Minutes
    Reading test - 5 passages and 52 questions

Section 2 – 35 Minutes
    Writing and Language test - 4 passages and 44 English usage questions

Section 3 – 25 Minutes
    20 math questions (5 of them free response) no calculator

Section 4 – 55 Minutes
    38 math questions (8 of them free response) with calculator

The Study Hall Test Preparation Book

Math on SAT and not ACT

Vertex of a Parabola

The **vertex** of a parabola is the point where the parabola crosses its axis of symmetry. If the coefficient of the x^2 term is positive, the vertex will be the lowest point on the graph, the point at the bottom of the "U"-shape. If the coefficient of the x^2 term is negative, the vertex will be the highest point on the graph, the point at the top of the "U"-shape.
The standard equation of a parabola is

Standard Form
$y = ax^2 + bx + c$

$y = -2x^2 + 4x + 1$
vertex for x coordinate is: $-b/2a$
so $-4/2(-2) = 1$

then plug in for x
$y = -2(-1)^2 + 4(1) + 1$
$y = -2 + 4 + 1 = 3$

so (1,3) is the vertex

Vertex Form
$y = a(x - h)^2 + k$

(h,k) is vertex
so (1,3)

$y = 2(x - 1)^2 + 3$

Completing the Square – when FOIL or factoring will not work
$ax^2 + bx + c = 0$
1. divide all terms by "a" –tthe coefficient of x^2
2. move the number term to the right side of the equation
3. complete the square on the left side and balance by adding the same value to the right side $(b/2)^2$
4. take the square root of both sides
5. subtract the number that remains on the left to find "x"

Examples:
$x^2 + 4x + 1 = 0$
$x^2 + 4x = -1$ $(b/2)^2 = (4/2)^2 = 4$
$x^2 + 4x + 4 = -1 + 4$
$(x + 2)^2 = 3$
$x + 2 = \sqrt{3}$
$x = \sqrt{3} - 2$

$5x^2 - 4x - 2 = 0$
$x^2 - 4/5x - 2/5 = 0$
$x^2 - 4/5x = 2/5$
$x^2 - .8 = .4$ $(b/2)^2 = (.8/2)^2 = .4^2 = .16$
$x^2 - .8 + .16 = .4 + .16$
$(x - .4)^2 = .56$
$x - .4 = \sqrt{.56}$
$x = \sqrt{.56} - .4$

Quadratic Formula

Often, the simplest way to solve "$ax^2 + bx + c = 0$ for the value of x is to factor the quadratic, set each factor equal to zero, and then solve each factor. But sometimes the quadratic is too messy, or it doesn't factor at all, or you just don't feel like factoring. While factoring may not always be successful, the Quadratic Formula can *always* find the solution.

The Quadratic Formula uses the "*a*", "*b*", and "*c*" from "$ax^2 + bx + c$", where "*a*", "*b*", and "*c*" are just numbers; they are the "numerical coefficients" of the quadratic equation they've given you to solve. The Quadratic Formula is derived from the process of completing the square, and is formally stated as:

$y = ax^2 + bx + c$ is the equation in standard form

Factoring is faster, so try first, but when factoring will not work

$$x = \frac{-b \pm \sqrt{b^2 - 4ac}}{2a}$$

The Study Hall Test Preparation Book

MATH CUES

You should recognize each of these math terms and symbols as cues to a type of problem the SAT is likely to be posing. We are referring mainly here to the less obvious questions, especially ones where figures aren't used, or when they are combined.

$\sqrt{2}$
When you see $\sqrt{2}$ in a question, look for a 45°/45° right triangle to be a part of the problem. Apply the 45°/45° rule (side – side - side$\sqrt{2}$) to the problem.

$\sqrt{3}$
If you see $\sqrt{3}$ in a question, there is usually a 30°/60° right triangle involved. Apply the 30°/60° rule (short side – short side$\sqrt{3}$ – twice the short side) to the problem.

π
If you see a π in the problem a circle or part of a circle is almost always involved.

60° - equilateral – congruent sides
They use these terms to indicate you have an equilateral triangle – 3 equal sides and 3 equal 60° angles.

Sides of a triangle with no angle given and no right triangle mentioned
If they present a problem where they want to know something about the lengths of the sides of a triangle and there are no angles given nor is there a right angle in the triangle, they want to know if you realize that the sum of the lengths of any 2 sides of a triangle must exceed the length of the third side.

3-4-5 (and 5-12-13) right triangles
These "triplets" – especially the 3-4-5 – show up all the time. They show up as 3-4-5, 6-8-10, etc. The ratio will be apparent.

Shaded regions in a geometric form
Remember that questions that want to know the area of a shaded region means you will have to subtract one geometric form from another.

Angles in a triangle without a right angle
If they ask a question about the angles and sides in a triangle that does not include a right triangle, the real question is if you know that larger angles generate longer sides.

Points on a graph
If they ask you for the distance between points on a graph, use the Pythagorean Theorem. Plot the points and determine the distances you can find subtracting along lines parallel to the x and y axes, then set up the Pythagorean Theorem.

Perpendicular lines – slope
Remember that the product of the slope of perpendicular lines is -1. This means the slope of one of the lines is the negative reciprocal of the other line. For example, a line perpendicular to a line with a slope of 2 would have a slope of -½.

The Study Hall Test Preparation Book

Slope
The slope of a line is determined by "rise over run" – the distance a line goes up divided by the distance a line goes across. Just say to yourself, "the line goes up _ and goes over_." A positive slope goes "up" from left to right. A negative slope goes "down" left to right. A line parallel to the x-axis has no slope.

Simultaneous Equations
When you see simultaneous equations in a question on this test, you must realize that it is crucial to look at your target. Focus on what you are looking for. Then look at the equations and see how you can manipulate the equations to get to that solution. To solve the problem you may need to add, subtract, combine, or take apart the equations.

"Wordy" problem
When you see a problem that looks like a big paragraph, realize two things.

First, the test makers usually use a lot of words (frequently used awkwardly as well) to distract you from a fairly easy problem.

Secondly, you must remember to get the numbers out of the words. Start writing the numbers down as you read the problem. Don't sit staring at the problem; start working it.

"one possible solution"
If you see "one possible solution" or "one possible answer" in the question, that means there are multiple answer choices to the question.

If this phrase is used in the student generated answer choice section, just solve the problem and bubble in one choice.

If you see the phrase in the multiple choice section, eliminate the 4 answer choices that will not work.

"could be"
When the test asks what "could be" means there are multiple answer choices that are possible.

If this phrase is used in the student generated answer choice section, just solve the problem and bubble in one choice.

If you see the phrase in the multiple choice section, eliminate the 4 answer choices that will not work.

"must be"
When you see this term you must realize that it means the answer has to always be true. They usually use this with some numeric trait, like a number being even or odd or being positive or negative.

The Study Hall Test Preparation Book

Combinations
When the combination is completely random you can use the factorial. (For instance, you are looking for how many combinations of the order of 5 classes are possible. That would be 5!
Or 5 x 4 x 3 x 2 x 1 = 120.

If they take the randomness out of the question by limiting the possibilities with some criteria, then look at the multiples that are possible for one instance. Take the value you arrive at and apply it to the other instances.

Abstraction – presence of variables instead of numbers
When the question is worded using variables instead of numeric values, the key to solving the problem is to substitute simple numbers in place of the variables. Set up the problem logically using the numbers, then substitute the variables back into the setup you have arrived at for the problem.

Change in average
Any problem that involves adding or subtracting a factor from an average, or the average increasing or decreasing, the solution lies in the totals. By that we mean multiply the average by the number of factors to get a total. Then see how the addition or subtraction affects the totals.

Percentages
When doing percentage problems, work with the percentages as decimals. Remember that if you are reducing a value you will be multiplying by a percentage less than 1.00. If you are increasing a value you multiply by a greater value than 1.00.

For example a 30% decrease would be 70% (.70) of the price. A 30% increase would be 130% (1.30) of the price.

Fraction in the denominator
If you see a fraction in the denominator of a fraction, remember that the fraction in the denominator "flips" so that you multiply the numerator by the reciprocal of the denominator.
As an example:
2/(1/3) = 2 x 3/1 = 6.

The Study Hall Test Preparation Book

SAT Idioms

capable	of	afflicted	with	abide	by
composed	of	argue	with	inspired	by
desirous	of	comply	with		
in search	of	consistent	with	insist	upon
partake	of	tamper	with		
resentful	of	associate	with	succeed	in
jealous	of	preoccupied	with	participate	in
threat	of	fascination	with	believe	in
consist	of	popular	with		
height	of	contrast	with		
approve	of	work	with		
in charge	of	provide	with		
responsibility	to	buy	from	rely	on
cater	to	different	from	depend	on
conform	to	divergent	from	count	on
intend	to	prohibit	from		
plan	to	separate	from	wait	for
oblivious	to	distinguish	from	provide	for
indebted	to	transition	from	excuse	for
try	to	recover	from	hope	for
related	to	hide	from		
required	to	escape	from		
opposition	to	different	from		
endeavor	to				
resort	to	dispute	over		
contribution	to	debate	over		
compare	to				
object	to	discriminate	against		
subscribes	to				
agreed	to	contrast	between		
contrast	to				
		in a world	where		
estimated	to be				
appears	to be				
believed	to be				
require	to be				

The Study Hall Test Preparation Book

Words that are Commonly Misused

accede / exceed

    Accede means to agree, to allow; exceed means to go beyond, to surpass, as in "Drivers who exceed the speed limit are asking for hefty fines."

accept / except

    Not commonly seen even from unpublished writers, who are probably familiar with the difference because they're all waiting for an acceptance!
    "We accept your invitation to your party, except for Bill, who will be away on that day."

adapt / adept / adopt

    Adapt means to adjust, adept means skilled and adopt means to take as your own:
    "Some people cannot adapt to new surroundings."
    "He is very adept at dodging awkward questions."
    "He tends to adopt the attitudes of those around him."

adverse / averse

    Adverse means inauspicious, hostile; averse means disinclined, repelled.
    "I'm very much averse to making a long, arduous journey under such adverse weather conditions."

advice / advise

    Advice is the noun and advise the verb.
    "His advice was that we should advise everybody to either stay away or be extremely careful."

affect / effect

    Affect is a verb; effect is more usually a noun. When used as a verb it means to achieve, fulfil, realise.
    "Bad weather will affect the quality of the fruit."
    "The effect of bad weather is a reduction in fruit quality."
    I can't think of any sentence using effect as a verb where one of the other three mentioned above wouldn't be a much better choice, but perhaps a politician might say, "To effect our goal of saving 10%…"

The Study Hall Test Preparation Book

aloud / allowed

Aloud means out loud, speaking so that someone else can hear you; allowed means permitted.

already / all ready

Already means by this time; all ready means prepared.
"Are you already packed?"
"Yes, I'm all ready to leave."

altogether / all together

Altogether means wholly; all together means everybody in a group:
"It's altogether too bad that you can't come."
"All together, now: 'Good morning, Sir!'"

all right / alright

All right is the correct form; alright is grammatically incorrect.

allude / elude

Allude means to refer to; elude means to dodge or escape.

allusion / illusion

Allusion is an indirect reference or hint; illusion means deception or mirage.

all ways / always

All ways means by every way or method; always means all the time, forever.

alternately / alternatively

Alternately is an adverb that means in turn; one after the other: "We alternately spun the wheel in the game." Alternatively is an adverb that means on the other hand; one or the other: "You can choose a large bookcase or, alternatively, you can buy two small ones."

among / between

Among always implies more than two, a group; between literally implies only two.

annual / annul

Annual means yearly; annul means to make void or invalid.

anyone / any one

This is quite tricky. Anyone means anybody, any person at all; any one means any one person and is followed by "of".
"Does anyone else want to come?"
"Any one of you is welcome to come along."

appraise / apprise

Appraise is to assess or estimate. Apprise is to inform or notify:
"I will appraise the situation and immediately apprise everybody of my conclusions."
Please don't make your character say or write anything like this, though—unless you want him to sound like a pompous twit!

ascent / assent

Ascent is an upward movement; assent means agreement.

assistance / assistants

Assistance means help or aid; assistants is the plural of assistant, one who gives help.

assure / ensure / insure

Assure means to guarantee; ensure means to make sure; insure means to protect against loss or damage:
"I assure you there's no call for alarm."
"To ensure your crockery doesn't get broken, wrap it all in bubble wrap."
"In case of breakage or loss, you should insure everything with a good insurance company."

The Study Hall Test Preparation Book

auger / augur

    Auger is a tool; augur means to predict.

baited / bated

    Baited usually refers to traps or snares. When the reference is to someone who is hardly daring to breathe, the correct word is always bated:
"She watched with bated breath."
I've yet to read that someone "bated a trap" instead of baiting it, but there's always a first time.

bare / bear

    Bare means naked; bear (apart from being a large animal) means to carry.

beside / besides

    Beside means by the side of; besides means in addition to.

biannual / biennial

    These two are really tricky! Biannual means happening twice a year; biennial means every two years.

blonde / blond

    Because these are borrowed from French there is a feminine and masculine form. Blonde is feminine and blond is masculine.

bore / boar / boor

    Bore as a noun is a boring or tiresome person, or something that you don't like doing; boar is a male pig; boor is a vulgar person.

board / bored

    Board is a long sheet of wood, also a group of people as in "Board of Directors", and as a verb means to go onto a ship, plane or other form of public transport; bored means not interested.

The Study Hall Test Preparation Book

born / borne

Born is always the beginning of life, borne means carried.
"I was born in the middle of a particularly severe winter."
"The logs were borne down the river to the mill."

bought / brought

Bought is the past tense of buy, brought is the past tense of bring. So, I bought (paid for) a load of topsoil, and a truck driver brought (delivered) it to my home.

braise / braze

Braise means to cook slowly in liquid (usually meat); braze most commonly means to solder with an alloy of copper and zinc.

brake / break

Brake means to stop; break means to smash.

bridal / bridle

Bridal has to do with brides and weddings; bridle as a noun means a halter or restraint; as a verb it means to restrain or to draw oneself up in anger.

by / buy / bye

By is a preposition meaning next to; buy means purchase; bye means farewell or good-bye.

canvas / canvass

Canvas is cloth or fabric; canvass means to seek votes, to survey, to sell door-to-door.

capital / capitol

Capital means the seat of government; money invested; excellent, as in "What a capital idea!". Capitol is the building where government meets, although in New Zealand that's simply called The Beehive.

caret / caret / carrot

A carat is a unit of weight for precious stones; a caret is a proof-reading symbol (^); a carrot is a vegetable

cite / site

Cite is a verb that means to quote as an authority or example: "I cited several eminent scholars in my study of water resources." It also means to recognize formally: "The public official was cited for service to the city." It can also mean to summon before a court of law: "Last year the company was cited for pollution violations." Site is a noun meaning location: "They chose a new site for the factory just outside town."

collaborate / corroborate

Collaborate means to work with someone; corroborate means to establish the truth of something.

compliment / complement

Compliment means praise or congratulate. You always pay someone a compliment, not a complement. Complement means to supplement, round out. Mustard complements ham, for instance, by "rounding out" the flavour.

comprise / compose

According to the traditional rule, the whole comprises the parts, and the parts compose the whole. Thus, the board comprises five members, whereas five members compose (or make up) the board. It is also correct to say that the board is composed (not comprised) of five members.

concurrent / consecutive

Concurrent is an adjective that means simultaneous or happening at the same time as something else: "The concurrent strikes of several unions crippled the economy." Consecutive means successive or following one after the other: "The union called three consecutive strikes in one year."

connote / denote

Connote is a verb that means to imply or suggest: "The word 'espionage' connotes mystery and intrigue." Denote is a verb that means to indicate or refer to specifically: "The symbol for 'pi' denotes the number 3.14159."

The Study Hall Test Preparation Book

conscience / conscious

Do not confuse conscience, the noun, with conscious, the adjective.

continual / continuous

Continual means something that happens frequently, with breaks between the occurrences. Continuous means something that happens without stopping!
"Continual interruptions distract me from writing."
"The continuous noise of the motor mower distracts me from writing."

convince / persuade

Strictly speaking, one convinces a person that something is true but persuades a person to do something. "Pointing out that I was overworked, my friends persuaded [not convinced] me to take a vacation. Now that I'm relaxing on the beach with my book, I am convinced [not persuaded] that they were right." Following this rule, convince should not be used with an infinitive.

co-operation / corporation

Co-operation (usually spelt without the hyphen in US English) means working together; corporation is a business organisation.

correspondence / correspondents

Correspondence is written communication; correspondents are those who write it.

council / counsel / consul

A council is an assembly, like a city council (councilor); counsel (noun, verb) refers to advice (counselor); a consul is a foreign service officer.

creak / creek

Creak is both a noun and a verb and means squeak or groan (for instance, rusty hinges and loose floorboards creak); creek is a noun and means a waterway or stream.

The Study Hall Test Preparation Book

credible / creditable

    Credible means believable; creditable means praiseworthy or deserving credit.

criteria / criterion

    Criterion is singular; criteria is plural.

curb / kerb

    Curb means to control, as in "curb your temper", while kerb is the edge of a footpath or sidewalk.

desert / dessert

    Desert means to abandon (and can also be a noun, meaning a wasteland); dessert is the sweet course of a meal.

device / devise

    Device is a noun, meaning a gadget or (particularly in writing terms) an invention; devise is a verb, meaning to invent or plot.

discreet / discrete

    Discreet means respectful, prudent; discrete means separate or detached from others.

disinterested / uninterested

    Disinterested is an adjective that means unbiased or impartial: "We appealed to the disinterested mediator to facilitate the negotiations." Uninterested is an adjective that means not interested or indifferent: "They seemed uninterested in our offer."

draft / draught

    Draft refers to the first writing of your novel or story (or any other document). You can also be drafted (enlisted or recruited) into the army, navy, etc.
    Draught is an air movement, a drink (as in "draught of ale") or refers to a horse (or other animal) used for pulling ploughs, etc (e.g., "draught horse").

The Study Hall Test Preparation Book

elicit / illicit

Elicit means to extract or draw out; illicit means not legal.

eminent / imminent

Eminent means distinguished, famous; imminent means near, close at hand.

emigrate / immigrate

Emigrate means "to leave a place of abode for residence in another country." Immigrate means "to come for permanent residence into a country of which one is not a native."

everyday / every day

Everyday means commonplace, ordinary; every day is used for something that happens daily.

everyone / every one

Everyone means every person in a group; every one means each person and is always followed by "of".
"Everyone needs to know how to swim."
"Every one of you should be able to swim."

fair / fare

Fair means average, good-looking, pale, unbiased (what a lot of meanings for one little word!); fare is the money you pay to go somewhere by bus, train, plane, taxi, etc. It can also refer to a passenger. As a verb it means do, as in:
"I didn't fare as well in my exams this year as I'd hoped."

farther / further

Farther is used for physical distance; further for non-physical. For instance:
The farther we walked the more hostile the terrain became.
I promised to give the plan further thought.

faze / phase

The most common error is the use of phase when the writer means faze. To faze someone is to fluster or confuse them, whereas phase is mostly used in reference to a stage in someone's life—though it can be a stage in almost anything else:
"Like most children, Danny's going through a phase of refusing to eat his vegetables."
"Nothing fazes my mother, who can produce a meal for unexpected guests at a moment's notice."

fewer / less

Less refers to value, degree, or amount; fewer refers to number, to the countable.

figuratively / literally

Figuratively is an adverb that means metaphorically or symbolically: "Happening upon the shadowy figure, they figuratively jumped out of their shoes." Literally is an adverb that means actually: "I'm not exaggerating when I say I literally fell off my chair." It also means according to the exact meaning of the words: "I translated the Latin passage literally."

flammable / inflammable

These two words are actually synonyms, both meaning easily set on fire. The highly flammable (inflammable) fuel was stored safely in a specially built tank. Use nonflammable to mean not flammable.

flare / flair

Flare means to flash or blaze and (as a noun) is a pyrotechnic device; flair means ability or skill.

flaunt / flout

To flaunt means to show off shamelessly: "Eager to flaunt her knowledge of a wide range of topics, Helene dreamed of appearing on a TV trivia show." To flout means to show scorn or contempt for: "Lewis disliked boarding school and took every opportunity to flout the house rules."

forbear / forebear

Forbear means to refrain from; forebear is an ancestor or forefather.

foreword / forward

Foreword is the preface in a book, usually written by someone who is not the author; forward means ahead, near the front.

forth / fourth

Forth means forward; fourth is after "third".

foul / fowl

Foul can mean dishonourable (by foul means), disgusting (a foul smell), entangle (rubbish dumped in the river can foul fishing lines); fowl is a bird.

found / founded

Found is the past tense of find; founded means started, as in "My great grandfather founded this company nearly a hundred years ago."

founder / flounder

In its primary sense founder means to sink below the surface of the water: "The ship foundered after colliding with an iceberg." By extension, founder means to fail utterly. Flounder means to move about clumsily, or to act with confusion. A good synonym for flounder is blunder: "After floundering through the first half of the course, Amy finally passed with the help of a tutor."

gibe / jibe

Gibe means to taunt; jibe means to agree, correspond or tally; in boating it means to shift the sails.

gorilla / guerrilla

Gorilla is a large ape; guerrilla is a particular kind of soldier.

The Study Hall Test Preparation Book

hail / hale

Hail means to greet or to come from (as in "She hails from Texas") and as a noun it is frozen raindrops; hale means healthy or (as a verb) to haul.

hanged / hung

A criminal is always hanged; a picture is hung:
"We hung the portrait where everybody could see it."
"John Smith was hanged yesterday at dawn."
Just remember, "I'll be hanged if they're going to hang me," and you won't forget the difference again!

herd / heard

Herd is a group of animals; heard is the past tense of hear.

here / hear

Here refers to a location (as in "over here"). Hear is always what your ears do. I can't see why writers should get confused here, but they must do because I have seen this more than once. (And, no, that's not a sample sentence!) I've even seen "Here! Here!" when the writer wasn't having a character call another character, but was expressing support for a real person!

historic / historical

In general usage, historic refers to what is important in history, while historical applies more broadly to whatever existed in the past whether it was important or not: "a historic summit meeting between the prime ministers;" "historical buildings torn down in the redevelopment."

hoard / horde

Hoard means to stockpile and as a noun it is a cache of stockpiled stuff; horde is a large group.

hole / whole

Hole is an opening; whole means complete.

The Study Hall Test Preparation Book

home / hone

In this case the error is always using "hone in" instead of "home in". Hone means to sharpen.

immemorial / immortal

Immemorial means ancient beyond memory (as in the cliché "since time immemorial"); immortal means deathless, eternal.

imply / infer

The writer or speaker implies; the reader or listener infers. Imply means "to suggest without stating"; Infer means "to reach a conclusion based upon evidence."

incredible / incredulous

Incredible means "too extraordinary to admit of belief." Incredulous means "inclined not to believe on slight evidence."

ingenious / ingenuous

Ingenious means "clever, resourceful," as "an ingenious device." Ingenuous means "open, frank, artless," as "ingenuous actions."

intolerable / intolerant

Intolerable; means tiring, onerous crushing; intolerant means biased, prejudiced. Someone cannot be intolerable of another's beliefs.

irregardless / regardless

There is no such word as irregardless; the correct word is regardless

its, / it's

This is confusing because possessives normally have an apostrophe, but in this case it's is short for it is and its is possessive—always.
"Its colour is green and it's quite beautiful."
Other possessives that don't have an apostrophe are theirs, hers, yours and his—though I doubt anyone is likely to try putting one in his!

later / latter

Later means afterwards; latter is the second of two things.
"Later that day we went for a walk."
"We have two choices. The latter is the more reliable, but the former would be cheaper."

lay / laid

This pair confuses writers almost more than any other.
"He lay on his bed." Although this sentence is past tense, "laid" would be incorrect and suggests he was laying eggs.
"She sighed as she laid the visitors' book beside the pen and lay back wondering if she would ever make an entry in it again."
In present tense the sentence would read, "She sighs as she lays the visitors' book beside the pen and lies back, wondering if she will ever make an entry in it again."
BUT "I sigh as I lay the visitors' book beside the pen and lie back, wondering if I will ever make an entry in it again."
(In practice, I would probably write I place/placed and she places/placed. It's so much less confusing, not to mention less repetitive!)
"It lay on the desk beside an open book." Present tense would read, "It lies on the desk beside an open book."
"Our hens lay every day."
"The hens laid ten eggs yesterday."

lead / led

Lead (pronounced led) is a heavy metal or (pronounced leed) the present tense of led. So:
"He opens the door for me and I lead the guests upstairs to their rooms."
"He opened the door for me and I led the guests upstairs to their rooms."

lend / loan

Lend is a verb meaning to give something temporarily to someone; loan is a noun, meaning the temporary transfer of something to someone else. So, "Dad, can you loan me a few dollars until pay day?" is incorrect.

The Study Hall Test Preparation Book

lessen / lesson

Lessen means to make less; lesson is something you learn.

liable / libel

Liable means subject to, answerable for or likely; libel is written (as opposed to spoken) untruths about someone, for which you may be taken to court.
"He is liable to sudden attacks of ill temper for no apparent reason."
"Politicians should be made liable for their bad decisions."
"Pollen is liable to cause hay fever or even asthma attacks in certain individuals."

lightening / lightning

Lightening means making lighter or brighter; lightning (which is always a noun) is what comes out of the sky, usually followed by a crack of thunder.

lose / loose

Lose always means mislaying or dropping something and not being able to find it, while loose means slack or free:
"If the fastening on your wrist-watch is loose (slack) you may lose your watch."

manner / manor

I saw this pair confused in an email ("all manor of complaints") and figured if one person could get them confused others could too. Manner means method, appearance, class, character; manor is strictly a large, stately house.

mantel / mantle

Mantel is the shelf above a fireplace, or the fireplace surrounding; mantle is a cloak or blanket.

marshal / marshall

Marshal is a military officer or a sheriff; marshall is a verb

maybe / may be

Another tricky one, best explained by demonstration:
"Maybe you could explain this to us a little clearer."
"It may be a good idea to give us a clearer explanation of this."

meet / mete / meat

The two more often confused are meet and mete. Meet means to encounter (and can also mean fit or suitable); mete means to allot, apportion or distribute; meat refers to flesh as food.

moral / morale

The noun moral means "lesson, maxim"; the adjective moral means "pertaining to right conduct, ethical." Morale, a noun, refers to "a cheerful, confident state of mind."

mute / moot

Mute as a verb means to silence or quieten down, as a noun it's a little gadget used by string players (particularly violinists) to soften the sound from their instruments. As an adjective it means dumb or making no sound, as in "He looked at me in mute appeal." Moot means debatable. So, it's a "moot point" not a "mute point".

no / know

Strange that these two should get confused, but they do. No is always the opposite of yes; know is to be certain (that you know the difference!)

overdo / overdue

It baffles me that people get these mixed up, but they do. Overdo means to exaggerate or carry something too far; overdue is what your bills are when you forget to pay them!

passed / past

Passed is the past tense of pass. Past means a time that has gone.
"Time passed and we all forgot the incident."
"In times past it was the custom for women to wear hats in church."

The Study Hall Test Preparation Book

peace / piece

Peace means the absence of war (or even noise); piece is a portion of something.

plain / plane

Plain means obvious, also unadorned or lacking in good looks; plane is a carpenter's tool or an abbreviation of aeroplane.

patience / patients

Patience means forbearance; patients are people under medical care.

peek / pique / peak

Pique means to excite or irritate; peek means to peep or snoop; peak as a noun means the summit or tip, and as a verb means to climax. So, you pique someone's curiosity; you don't peek or peak it. If someone annoys you, you become piqued rather than peeked or peaked.

penultimate

Meaning "next to last," penultimate is often mistakenly used to mean "the very last," or the ultimate: "The perfectionist was crestfallen when he was awarded the penultimate prize; the grand prize went to another."

pour / pore

You pour sauces, gravies, etc, over your dinner, while pore means to study something—so, "pore over the book", not "pour over the book", which reads as though you might be damaging the book with an unnamed liquid substance!

precede / proceed

The verb precede means to come before. Proceed means to move forward. "He preceded me into the room; once I caught up with him I proceeded to tell him off."

The Study Hall Test Preparation Book

premise / premises

Premise usually means assumption, supposition, while premises means an apartment, house or building and its grounds.

presence / presents

Presence means being near at hand; presents are gifts.

principal / principle

Principal means chief or main, also the amount borrowed in a loan; principle means regulations or ideals.
"The principal reason for the company's failure was lack of money." (or)
"The new principal is making a real difference to our school."
"We are paying both principal and interest each month on our mortgage."
"She is completely without principles and would steal from her own mother."
"The principle of a clause like this in your employment contract is to protect you against unfair dismissal."

quiet / quite

Quiet means without noise; quite when used in fiction usually means moderately, but can also mean totally or entirely. Use of the wrong word here could, of course, simply be a typing error that went unnoticed in the proof-reading stages!

rain / reign / rein

Rain is the water that comes down from clouds; reign means to rule; rein is a strap, usually leather, for controlling an animal, especially a horse.

raise / raze

These two are exact opposites. Raise means to lift or build up and raze means to pull down:
"We will raise the reputation of our village to new heights."
"He instructed his army to raze the village to the ground."

reality / realty

Reality is real life; realty is real estate.

The Study Hall Test Preparation Book

reference / reverence

I don't know if this confusion is common. I didn't even realise the words could be confused until I saw one wrongly used in something written by … a writer! Maybe it was just a typing error. Reference is something referred to, reverence means respect.

regimen / regiment

Regimen is a noun and is mostly used to refer to to a prescribed way of life, or diet or exercise. It is also the action of governing. Regiment as a verb means to direct, command; as a noan it refers to a military unit.

residence / residents

Residence is a house; residents are the people who live there.

respectfully / respectively

Respectfully means politely; respectively means in the order stated.
"The containers stood in a row and were numbered 1, 3, 2, 5 and 4 respectively" means they were standing in this order rather than numerical order.

retch / wretch

Retch means to gag or try to vomit; wretch is a grovelling person, a creep.

rifle / riffle

Rifle (apart from being a firearm) means to steal; riffle means to leaf through or browse. So your character doesn't rifle through someone's belongings and only rifles them if stealing them.

right / rite / write

Right means correct; rite is a ceremony, usually religious; write means to make words.

road / rode

Road is a long surface for cars and other vehicles; rode is the past tense of ride.

The Study Hall Test Preparation Book

sale / sail

    Sale is either offering something for purchase ("for sale") or offering it at a special price ("on sale"); sail is part of a ship or boat.

scene / seen

    Scene is the place where something happens; seen is the past participle of see.
"Yet he had seen nothing suspicious at the scene of the accident." (Of course you wouldn't write a sentence like that; the two words make for a clumsy combination. I would probably replace "scene" with "site".)

seam / seem

    Seam is most often used to refer to the joining of two pieces of fabric with thread, but it can refer to other types of joins; seem means appear: "He makes it seem so easy to do."

sell / cell

    Sell is to exchange for money; cell is a small room (invariably lacking in comfort); also an organism (as in "stem cells"); the small divisions in something large such as a container or a table in a web page or word-processed document.

shear / sheer

    Shear means to cut or clip; sheer means transparent (as in "sheer nylon hosiery"); steep (as in "a sheer drop"); total or absolute (as in "sheer stupidity").

serf / surf

    Serf means slave or servant; surf is a wave and as a verb is also the action of riding the waves on a board or using a computer to find something on the Internet.

shore / sure

    Shore as verb means to brace or support; as a noun it is usually a beach but can also be a support or a brace; sure means certain, confident. So you do not sure up a company by borrowing more capital; you shore it up.

site / sight / cite

Site always refers to location or place: building site; archaeology site.
"We will site the house to take advantage of the panoramic views."
Sight always refers to vision, as in the cliché "a sight for sore eyes".
"We sighted two horsemen coming over the hill."
"It was a sight I would never forget."
"She feared she might lose her sight."
Cite means to summon, or to refer to a source, as in the following sentences:
"I was cited as a witness to the accident."
"He cited in his defence an incident in which these same people were involved."

some time / sometime

This is a common confusion. Some time is a period of time and sometime means at some time not specified.
"Some time ago you promised to introduce me to your brother."
"Sometime when you're not busy we must do this again."

stationary / stationery

Stationary means standing still. Stationery refers to writing paper.

statue / statute / stature

Statue is a carved or moulded likeness; statute is law; stature means height or status.

straight / strait

Straight means without bends; strait is a passage of water.

taut / taught / taunt

Taut means tight, firm; taught is the past tense of teach; taunt equals jeer, insult.

tenant / tenet

Tenant is one who rents a property; tenet is a principle or belief.

there / their / they're

There is a location: "Put it over there."
Their is the possessive of they: "their coats"
They're is short for they are: "They're unlikely to miss seeing them."
So: "They hung their coats over there by the door where they're unlikely to miss seeing them on their way out." Dreadful sentence I know, but at least it demonstrates the correct usage for all three words.

to / too / two

To is a preposition meaning towards; too means also or extremely (as in "You are walking too fast for me"); two is the number after one.

vane / vain / vein

Vane is something that shows from which direction the wind is blowing; also (among other things) the sail of a windmill, the flat part on either side of the shaft of a feather, a revolving fan or flywheel; vain means too concerned about how one looks (though one can be vain about other things, of course!) and also means useless, as in "a vain attempt"; vein is a blood vessel, a channel. When you blaspheme you are "taking the Lord's name in vain".

venal / venial

Venal means dishonest, dishonourable; venial means forgivable, unimportant (as in "venial sins").

vicious, / viscous

Vicious means savage, cruel; viscous means thick, gummy.

waist / waste

Waist is the part of your body around which you fasten your belt; waste as a noun mostly refers to stuff that's thrown away. As a verb it usually means to squander.

wary / weary

Wary means careful; weary means tired.

The Study Hall Test Preparation Book

wave / waive

Wave means to flap your hand in farewell and as a noun is also a breaker on the beach; waive means to give up one's rights or claim.

waver / waiver

Waver means to be undecided; waiver means the giving up of rights or claims.

weak / week

Weak is the opposite of strong; week is seven days, Sunday to Saturday.

wet / whet

Wet as a verb means strictly to pour liquid on something. You do not "wet" somebody's appetite for anything; you'll only land up doing the opposite of what you want! Instead, you whet it, which means to sharpen or stimulate.

which / witch

As a fantasy writer, I have trouble believing people get these two confused! Which is one of a group; witch is a sorcerer.

whose / who's

This confusion is similar to its and it's. Whose is possessive, and who's is short for "who is".

yoke / yolk

Yoke as a verb means to bind or confine. In olden days, for instance, oxen were yoked together for ploughing. As a noun it is more usually the means by which something is bound or confined, though I remember the upper part of a two-piece bodice on a dress or blouse being referred to as a yoke. Yolk is the yellow part of an egg.

your / you're

Your is the second person possessive adjective, used to describe something as belonging to you. *Your* is nearly always followed by a noun. *You're* is a contraction of "you are" and is often followed by the present participle (verb form ending in -ing).

Made in the USA
San Bernardino, CA
05 July 2016